Performance Coaching

Skills-Based Strategies for Developing Self-Propelled People

John Brantley

Benson & Latimer Press

DANIELSVILLE, GEORGIA

First Printing, June 2003
Revised Edition, February 2006

Requests for information should be addressed to:

Benson & Latimer Publishing, P.O. Box 378, Danielsville, GA 30633
Telephone: 706-795-3557 Fax: 706-534-2307
Email: jtbcommunications@alltel.net

ISBN 0-9707682-3-0

This book is dedicated to
Patty Brantley,
my wife and companion for twenty-five
years. You have been a constant source
of encouragement and support.
I love you.

Thanks.

Foreword

The term "coaching" is the most popular term associated with leadership in this first decade of the new millennium. As more and more organizations move to a "team" orientation, the role of the leader as a coach becomes more and more critical.

Unfortunately, we have found that many leaders struggle with how to coach effectively. The problem is usually in two areas: mindset and mechanics.

Many leaders do not see developing staff as a core responsibility. These leaders usually believe that their staff should be able to read their mind and act accordingly without guidance and direction.

The struggle for other leaders is understanding how to coach. These leaders are developing the right mindset, but they struggle with "how to do it." The purpose of this book is to help leaders develop the right mindset and teach leaders how to effectively coach their people to improve performance.

We hope that in some small way, this book will help you be more effective at coaching your staff. When coaching improves, so does the performance of the organization and each individual in the organization. It is the most important role that a leader has!

John T. Brantley

Acknowledgements

This book is the culmination of many years of work in the field of performance coaching. There are many people who have played a part in bringing these ideas to print.

Special thanks to Deborah Owensby, who has tolerated my crazy behavior with graciousness.

Nell Whalen and Janice Miller both graciously edited the manuscript and provided valuable suggestions. Thanks for your hard work.

Ken Parker and Gus Whalen, my close friends, have encouraged me for years to put the performance coaching process in print. Thank you for your encouragement.

I would finally like to thank my clients who have been the laboratory for developing this performance coaching process. Specifically, I would like to thank John Weller, the late Jerry Morgan, Wayne Thiessen, and many others for the opportunity to teach this process across the United States.

Professionally, I would like to thank Becky Keenum, Johnny Terrell, Chris Maddox and many others who have provided insight and encouragement along the journey.

John Brantley

Table of Contents

Section I

The Foundation

High performing people are the "life-blood" of every organization. Getting results is impossible without them. Great products and services are useless without motivated people to sell and deliver them to your customers in a timely manner. The best technology is of little value without the right people to use the technology. Quality customer service hinges on having high performers.

Most people, though, do not possess all of the characteristics you desire when you hire them. Your responsibility as a leader is to develop your people into the type of self-propelled people that you need in your organization.

CHAPTER ONE

Self-Propelled People

*If you don't know your target, you will
never know when you hit it.*

The self-propelled lawnmower

As a child, going to Mama and Papa's house was a major treat.
Mama and Papa were my maternal grandparents. They lived on a
twenty-acre farm that provided an endless stream of adventure and
exploration.

Papa was a self-educated, mechanical wizard who could build virtually anything. He also had asthma, which limited his physical exer-
tion. Because of this, he was particularly interested in mechanical
contraptions that would make hard work easier.

As a teenager, the contraption, which captivated my interest, was a
self-propelled lawnmower. I was just at the age where cutting grass
was a sign of maturing. It was a "manly" thing to do. I had already
been cutting grass for a couple of years in our hilly yard at home. It

was pure drudgery pushing a lawn mower up the hill or holding it back coming down the hill. Going up the hill was like pushing a steam locomotive up a mountain. Coming down the hill was like trying to hold that same steam locomotive back. Mowing was different at Papa's house. Papa had the first lawnmower that I had ever seen that propelled itself. It was a big, heavy, green Sears and Roebuck self-propelled lawnmower. It was truly amazing. All you had to do was check the oil and gas, crank it, engage the clutch to the drive system, and walk behind it. No pushing, no shoving, no holding back - just steering. The rest was automatic. It was just like heaven to me.

Self-propelled people – What every leader wants

In the workshops and seminars that we teach, I have come to realize that every leader wants the human version of that self-propelled lawnmower – self-propelled people. Leaders want a workforce of people who can basically guide their own work performance: self-starters who possess all of the essential skills, knowledge and characteristics needed to be successful. Think about your star performers. What do you like about them? Most of your comments will fall into four categories: attitude, initiative, skills and perseverance. They are focused on success and take the initiative to achieve success. They have the necessary skills and knowledge, and they persist in using these skills until they succeed. In short, they exhibit the self-starter characteristics you are seeking in your people.

Think about the people that frustrate you. What frustrates you about them? Most likely your comments will fall into the same four categories: attitude, initiative, skills and perseverance. They have a negative attitude or a "don't care" attitude. You constantly have to monitor their performance or tell them what to do. They either lack the skills for success or they are not willing to use their skills. What-

ever the reasons for their lack of action, they do not exhibit these
self-starter characteristics that you want and need in your people.

Self-propelled people –
An essential part of the workplace today

Self-propelled people are not just what leaders want, though. Self-
propelled people are what the workplace demands today. The
workplace is very fast and complex today. One leader or even a
group of leaders cannot control everything. The intense demand for
customer focus, teamwork, improving productivity, and managing
cost means that every person must be actively thinking and acting in
the best interest of the organization. Reflect on your organization.
How would your organization benefit if everyone were focused on
customer satisfaction, controlling costs and working together? If
you are like my clients, the impact would be astronomical. Self-
propelled people are essential for success today.

Self-propelled people –
The dilemma and the good news

Unfortunately, leaders face a dilemma. Everyone does not exhibit
these self-propelled traits. If they did, there would be no need for
this book or most of the other books on leadership written today.
Leaders react to this dilemma in a number of ways. Some wring
their hands in despair. Some seek to "over control" their people to
get results. Others give up and say, "You just can't get good help
any more." If you are not ready to give up on your people, there is
good news. Even though most people do not come to you with all of
the attitude and skills you desire, most can develop them. While
every person in your organization may not be able to make this transition, 85-95% can with proper guidance and direction.

The key is the phrase – "proper guidance and direction." As you will learn in the next chapters, most people do not naturally possess all of the skills, knowledge, and beliefs of the self-propelled person. Most can, however, develop the skills, knowledge and beliefs if they are given effective guidance and coaching over a period of time. To get people to the level of performance that you desire, there is "some assembly required." Developing self-propelled people will not happen by osmosis, luck, or having the right karma. Developing self-propelled people requires following a predictable process and using the right process over time.

That is the purpose of this book - to show you how to guide, direct and coach your people so they can become the self-propelled people you desire. The first step in the process is to clearly define the type of people you desire.

It all begins with a clear target

Have you ever played Pin the Tail on the Donkey? It was a classic birthday party game when I was growing up. The rules are very simple. The goal of the game is to successfully pin the tail on a picture of a donkey (minus the tail) that is placed on a wall a few feet from you. The only catch is that you are blindfolded and then turned around two or three times before you begin. It is a hilarious game to watch. The person who is blindfolded is not certain if the tail is being placed on the head of the donkey, the tail of the donkey, or even close to the donkey.

The workplace today is often like a game of Pin the Tail on the Donkey. In some cases leaders are not clear on exactly what they desire in their people. These leaders have an idea of what they want but nothing specific. They have never defined their target behavior and never developed a specific plan to reach the target behavior. These leaders are guessing at success. They know approximately where the target is, but they really don't know if they are taking the correct actions to develop self-propelled people.

In other cases, leaders know what they want, but they do not clearly communicate this to their people. In these situations, the people in the organization are like the blindfolded person, constantly trying to guess if they are doing things right. Both situations lead to much frustration and loss of productivity.

Performance Coaching Principle #1

To develop self-propelled people you must have a clear understanding of what a self-propelled person looks and acts like.

The first step to eliminate this frustration and develop self-propelled people is to have a clear understanding of your target – the type of people that you want in your organization. This first step is the most critical step in the entire process. If you develop a clear understanding of what you are expecting from people in your organization, communicate this effectively, and reinforce it over time, you will be amazed at how many of your people begin acting just like you desire.

<u>Self-propelled people - Clearly defining your target</u>

It sounds simple, doesn't it! Here are two simple steps to start you on the journey to developing self-propelled people in your organization.

- Step One - List the characteristics, behavior skills, knowledge and beliefs that someone must have to be successful in your organization or in their role. Be as specific as possible.

- Step Two - Beside each characteristic, skill, behavior, knowledge and belief, list at least three observable behaviors that describe this characteristic or skill. Example: Initiative is a common characteristic that leaders seek in their people. List at least three different behaviors that communicate to you that someone is taking initiative. You might list behaviors like the following: prioritizes daily work assignments without being told to do so; initiates conversation with co-workers to solve problems; communicates with leaders if there are problems outside of his or her control.

By doing step two, you are clearly defining the behavior that you seek in your people. It is much easier to communicate this expectation if you know specifically what you seek.

Do I really have to be this specific?

Leaders will frequently ask, "Do I really have to be this specific? Shouldn't they understand this on their own?" The worst mistake you can make is to talk in "shoulds and oughts." Whether your people "should" understand or not is irrelevant if they are not doing it! If you want self-propelled people you must be specific in your expectations. If people have to guess what your expectations are, you increase the possibility that their understanding of success will be different than yours. When this happens, you are in trouble.

Action Step

If you are serious about developing self-propelled people, follow the steps listed above and define the specific type of people that you desire in your organization.

CHAPTER TWO

Stop Pushing and Pulling

Pushing or pulling people is a waste of time and energy.

When the self-propelled lawnmower did not work

In early August of my fourteenth year, I went to Papa's to again cut grass. The heat and Papa's asthma made it out of the question for him to cut grass that day. When I went to the garage to pull out the lawnmower, I was horrified to discover that the drive gear was broken and I would have to push the lawnmower. Do you know how hard it is to push a self-propelled lawnmower? It is like trying to run in a swimming pool. The gearbox itself must weigh 30 pounds, and the whole mower weighed well over 100 pounds. Pushing it up a steep slope was absolute torture. Never in all of my life have I worked so hard to cut grass.

The leader's frustration

This same type of frustration is what leaders have verbalized in Performance Coaching workshops for years. Their frustration lies in having to push or pull people when they really believe people should be self-propelled. They feel just like I did pushing that lawnmower up a hill.

Unfortunately, leaders who have to push or pull people to get results are caught in a vicious cycle. The leader feels the need to push or pull to get results. The people react with resentment and frustration. They resist being pushed or pulled. The people complain of being treated like children. The leader is compelled to watch them like children. The leader gets frustrated and expresses displeasure. The people feel devalued and express their feelings by slowing down or taking even less action on their own. This increases the leader's frustration. In the end everyone is exhausted, and the leader has people who do not act on their own but wait instead for the leader to tell them what to do.

You must do something different

Performance Coaching Principle #2

If you want people to become self-propelled, you must do something different.

If you are serious about helping your people become self-propelled and if you are tired of pushing or pulling, you must do something different. While this may state the obvious, it is an obvious that many leaders miss. Many leaders think that to develop self-propelled people they have to just try harder at what they are doing. "I just need to give a little more effort," they will say. "I just need to push harder!" Usually the problem with leaders is not in the level of effort they make or their intent. Most people have good intentions. The problem usually is that they are doing the wrong things.

The first step you must take is to stop pushing or pulling. This behavior is resented by your people and it is exhausting to you. It is impossible (and I repeat IMPOSSIBLE!) to develop self-propelled people by pushing or pulling.

Pushing and pulling are out of sync with today's work culture

When I was in my twenties I came across a picture of my dad's high school basketball team. I was stunned. I had played basketball myself in high school but never knew that my dad played the game. A marvelous conversation ensued. "Yes, son, I played basketball. I was the master of the two-hand set shot." It took me a second to realize what dad was talking about. Then I remembered. When I was a kid dad would sometimes come out and shoot baskets with me. He would always use the two-hand set shot. A hand was placed on each side of the ball and the ball was pushed up from the chest. I always thought it was a funny way to shoot. I had been taught to shoot with one hand behind the ball, one hand in front of the ball and to shoot with the arms extended up. In our discussion I learned that the two-handed set shot was the way everyone shot a basketball then. Even the greatest of the pros of that era used the same approach. It was a very effective shot then.

Would the two-handed set shot work today in basketball? Not at all. Basketball is a more aggressive sport today. Most players are taller than when my father played. Virtually every "two-hand set shot" today would be blocked. What worked fine sixty years ago would be ineffective today.

The same principle is true with organizations and leadership styles. Pushing, controlling and manipulating may have worked a few years ago, but they just don't work today. Things have changed. The workplace and people have changed.

Most leaders who push or pull today to get results learned their leadership skills in an authoritarian culture. Until the eighties, most organizations were centralized, authoritarian cultures. In this culture, the leader was king (or queen). The role of the leader was to use control and authority, or any means necessary, to get results. Pressure, manipulation, intimidation, pushing and pulling were acceptable if they got results. The leader was the one who made decisions and told people what to do. Control was always in the hands of the leader. People were expected to do what they were told, don't ask questions, don't rock the boat and make their leader look good.

In the eighties, organizations began to change. Pressure to be competitive and the changing needs of employees caused organizations to begin the evolution toward a team-oriented culture. The team culture is fundamentally different than the authoritarian, control-oriented culture. In the team culture decisions are made at the lowest appropriate level, information is freely shared, people are involved in decision making and problem solving, clear lines of accountability are defined, and people are expected to think on the job.

This type of culture naturally requires a different style of leadership if it is to achieve optimum success. The authoritarian style of leadership is as out of place in the workplace today as the two-handed set shot is in the NBA. It just doesn't work.

What is a leader to do?

If you are not pushing or pulling, then what is the leader to do? To develop self-propelled people, you must replace pushing and pulling with effective coaching. Clear expectations, proper training, genuine caring, constant feedback, and accountability are the characteristics of effective coaching.

Pushing and pulling imply that people could do it if they really wanted to. Pushing and pulling imply that people have all of the skills and knowledge needed to be successful. The underlying assumption of pushing and pulling is that people are inherently lazy. They have the skills; they just are not using them. Effective coaching implies that the person has the capability to succeed and that most people want to succeed. Effective coaching implies that for people to use their skills and knowledge, they must be motivated to use them. Coaching recognizes that the key responsibility of the leader is to teach and guide employees until they can achieve the desired level of performance on their own.

The purpose of the coach

To help people develop the beliefs, knowledge and skills necessary to be successful in their jobs and to reinforce in a positive way these skills, knowledge and beliefs until the person or team achieves success

In the coaching role leaders must help their staff develop the skills and confidence to act successfully on their own.

The goal of coaching

The goal of effective coaching is well trained, self-motivated individuals and teams that are consistently performing at a successful level. In essence, the goal is to create self-propelled people. The goal of the coach is not to control the person's behavior. The goal is to make sure that the person has the ability to control and manage his or her own behavior.

Misconceptions about coaching

There are many misconceptions about what a coaching style of leadership is. Here are the most common.

Confusing "being nice" with effective coaching

Many people mistake "being nice" with effective coaching. It is always important to respect and value your people. This is an important part of effective coaching. Coaching, however, is fundamentally different from being nice to someone. In the spirit of being nice to people, some leaders avoid dealing with issues which should be addressed.

Backing off

This is a pattern that many leaders develop when they first try to change their leadership style. The old "I am the boss" is not acceptable anymore, but leaders are confused about what to do. In the confusion, they do nothing. They back off and assume that people understand what needs to be done and will do it on their own. The problem with this approach is that your people are as confused as you are. Most people react to what the leader does. If they see that you are not involved, they will become confused and not know what to do. They will become hesitant, or they will begin to exhibit "self-preservation" behavior.

What exactly is a coach supposed to do?

Many people espouse the importance of coaching. Most people, though, still struggle with how to coach. We will conclude this chapter with a brief understanding of the steps to effective coaching. First, remember the goal: to develop self-propelled people who are well-trained, self-motivated individuals and teams that are consistently performing at a successful level. With the goal in mind, here are the essential actions the coach must take:

- Clearly define goals and expectations so people know the target.
- Understand people so you know what is important to them and what motivates them.
- Help them develop the skills, knowledge and beliefs essential to success.
- Observe their behavior so you know whether they are achieving the desired goals.
- Reinforce positive behavior so they have a clear understanding of the right behavior.
- Address problem behavior quickly and in a problem solving way so they can learn from their mistakes and move forward.
- Help your people learn to track their performance so that they can consistently perform at the desired level.

Action Step

Review the performance problems you wish to correct with your people. Identify in each case, the actions you need to do differently if you want them to act differently.

CHAPTER THREE

What You Need to Know About People

Most people have the capability to be successful. They just need some guidance and direction.

What really makes the self-propelled lawnmower work?

For two long hours I sweated and groaned as I pushed the lawnmower up, down, and across Papa's front yard without the self-propelled gears working. Finally, exhausted, I stopped and went inside for some tea. I sat down next to Papa and said, "Boy, that lawnmower sure is a pain to push when the self-propelled part does not work." Papa looked surprised.

"It's not working now?" Papa asked.

"Nope, hasn't worked all day."

"Why didn't you tell me before you began cutting?" Papa asked. I mumbled some answer about how I thought he was busy. "Go get the mower and lets see if we can understand what is wrong."

That conversation ushered in a whole new understanding for me. I pushed the lawnmower into the garage, and we lifted it onto the workbench. Papa took a screwdriver and removed the cover from the gearbox. He peered into the box and then turned to me and smiled. "I could have saved you a lot of sweat if you had just checked with me first." The chain had simply fallen off of the gear. With just a slight adjustment it was back in place and running like new. While Papa had the cover off, he also decided that it would be a good time to help me understand how the whole thing worked. It only took ten minutes, but it gave me a new appreciation for a self-propelled lawnmower.

Why do people not push themselves?

Pushing and pulling by the leader occur because people are not willing to do something on their own. If you want self-propelled people, you have to get them to push themselves. If you assume that people are simply lazy, you miss the opportunity to help them develop their potential. The answer is more complex than laziness. The 10/80/10 principle will help you understand why some people do not push themselves.

Performance Coaching Principle #3

The 10/80/10 Principle – In an average group of people, approximately 10% come pre-assembled with all of the skills, knowledge and characteristics desired. Eighty percent (80%) are adapters who possess part of the skills, knowledge and characteristics and need some assembly. Ten percent (10%) are "unassemblable" (They are not going to be successful regardless of what you do.).

The 10/80/10 principle says that only about 10% of the people in most organizations possess all of the skills, knowledge and beliefs you desire them to have. These are the people who naturally push themselves. The other 90% are not going to naturally push themselves to the degree that most leaders desire.

The First Ten Percent – Pre-assembled (self-starters)

Only about 10% of the people in most organizations come to the organization with all of the skills, knowledge and characteristics you are seeking. We call these people "pre-assembled" because you must do very little to help them be successful. These persons will usually have the following characteristics:

- They take the initiative to learn on their own.
- They only have to be told once when given instructions or directions.
- They take initiative to solve problems on their own.
- They manage their own time and tasks without having to be told to do so.
- They initiate conversations to gain understanding.
- They anticipate issues and problems and take appropriate action to get the desired results.
- They evaluate and modify their own performance to achieve desired results.
- They are not only thinking about the task that is in front of them, but they are thinking about the implications of their task on others and on the future.
- They are constantly thinking about what is in the best interest of the organization.
- They have confidence in their own abilities.
- They learn from their mistakes and move forward.
- They do not stop until they have achieved their goals.

These "pre-assembled" self-starters possess two key elements. They have the skills, knowledge and beliefs needed to succeed, and they have the desire to use these skills, knowledge and beliefs without having to be told to do so. They push themselves.

In Performance Coaching seminars around the world, leaders have consistently identified that approximately 10% of their people have all of the skills, knowledge and characteristics that they desire. In some cases it may be more than 10% and in other cases it may be less, but usually around 10 % possess all of the characteristics you are seeking.

Think for a moment about the people in your organization. What percentage would you call true "pre-assembled" self-starters? If you have more than ten percent, congratulate yourself. You either have done a great job of coaching or you have an extra large percentage of natural self-starters. (You should thank God you are so fortunate!)

Look at the list you developed at the end of Chapter One. Compare this list to the characteristics of "pre-assembled" self-starters listed above. Are they similar? Almost all leaders, whether they are the CEO or a first line supervisor, will describe these "pre-assembled" self-starters as the people they desire in their organizations. They will also seek these characteristics whether they are hiring a vice president or a teller.

The most important thing to understand about your people is this – in most groups, only about ten percent naturally possess the skills, knowledge and beliefs you desire. This will vary slightly depending on the education level of your people and other factors. It is unrealistic and poor leadership to expect everyone to exhibit the skills, knowledge and beliefs without effective guidance and direction. Such poor leadership is like expecting every child to play the piano as a child prodigy would. The child prodigy's brain is wired differently.

For whatever reason, the prodigy came to the planet with more knowledge and skill related to the piano. However, there are many people who are capable of playing the piano with similar precision and skill as the prodigy. To achieve this level of performance, though, they must be taught and they must practice, practice, practice.

The Last Ten- Percent – "Unassembable" – Unsuccessful regardless of what you do

The last ten percent refers to the people in your organization who are not going to be successful, regardless of what you do. This may sound rather harsh, but it is not intended to be so. It is simply meant to reflect reality. Leaders would like for everyone to be successful. Unfortunately, that is not reality. For some reason, some people appear to have a built-in failure mechanism that causes them to stumble every time they get close to success. These people usually lack the skills needed to be successful or the desire to learn and apply the skills. In some cases, they are incapable of developing and using the skills because of past history, upbringing, self-destructive behaviors, or other related patterns. You can do everything possible for these people, and they will probably not be successful until they change something internally.

The Eighty Percent – Adapters – Some assembly required

The 80% in the middle of the 10/80/10 principle are the most important part of the principle. This 80% are what we call "adapters." They are the masses of the workforce. They possess some of the characteristics, skills and knowledge that you desire but not all of them. For these people to be successful, there is "some assembly required." They are called "adapters" because they will adapt to their work environments and to the expectations leaders have for them. They can rise to greatness or they can flounder in mediocrity.

The key is how they are led. These people, on a regular basis, check the direction of the organization and adapt to what they believe is really important to the organization. The word "really" should be emphasized at this point. These "adapters" continually assess what their leaders want and seek to comply. They are going to follow the leader's lead whether it is good or bad. For example, if they believe that the leader really wants quality, they will deliver quality. If they really believe that the leader wants quantity, rather than quality, they will deliver quantity regardless of what the posters in the building say about quality being #1. In short, this group is going to go where they think the organization wants them to go based on what they see from their direct supervisor.

This does not mean that they are bad or poor workers. Actually, it is quite the contrary. They are usually average to good workers. It is also important to understand that this group wants to be successful. Most of these people have the ability to exhibit self-propelled characteristics if they are coached properly. What is different about this group from the self-starters is that they are not going to do it on their own. They need guidance and direction to achieve success. There are a number of reasons for this. It may be lack of skills, lack of confidence, conflict avoidance, fear of failure, lack of direction or a variety of other reasons. Whatever the reason, they wait to take action until they get a nudge, or possibly two or three nudges. If they get consistent signals in the right direction, however, they will move right where you want them to go.

The most important thing for leaders to understand about this group of people is that they need a different style of leadership than the people who are self-starters. The biggest mistake leaders make is trying to lead the 80% like they lead the 10% who are self-starters. This dooms the leader and his or her people to frustration and often to failure. Here is why.

Self-starters, the first 10%, require little supervision and guidance.

They want you to tell them what needs to be done and then get out of their way. If they have questions, they will get back with you. They will take the initiative to be successful. You have to do little to help them. They will solve their own problems and develop their own strategies for success. They will track their progress and make adjustments as necessary.

The eighty percent, however, are not going to be as aggressive at accomplishing tasks and taking action on their own. You may have to explain parts of the task more than once. They may be afraid to say that they do not understand because they do not want to appear ignorant. Because of this you have to spend more time clarifying tasks in the beginning. They are not going to exhibit a certain behavior until it is consistently reinforced by you. With the eighty percent, you have to be more specific and follow-up more often to evaluate their performance. You must establish a feedback time so they can report back to you about the outcome. This pattern will need to be repeated numerous times before it becomes habit. The eighty percent need much more affirmation to be sure that they are on the right path.

Do you see the difference between the two? If you are treating the 80% like the self–starter 10% you will become frustrated when they don't "get it" the first time. You will have the tendency to start pushing or pulling. If you recognize that they need a different style of leadership, you can resist the temptation to push or pull.

In reality, the pattern of clarifying communication and establishing follow-up plans is something that should be done with all people, but the eighty percent need this reinforcement to really develop self-propelled skills and characteristics.

The 80% group is the focus of this book. The top 10% are already self-propelled. The bottom 10% are not going to be self-propelled because they lack the ability, desire or confidence to be self-directed.

The 80% section is where your energy should be focused as a leader. Kevin Thigpen, a Human Resource executive in Athens, Georgia, illustrated that point to me one day. Kevin said that he and the managers in his organization were trying to figure out how to better use their time as leaders. They began to track how they spent their time, particularly in relation to coaching employees. When they looked at the data, they were surprised. They realized that most of their coaching time was spent with the ten percent of the workforce that were not going to be successful. They were spending eighty percent of their time with the ten percent of the workforce that would not be there in the next twelve to eighteen months. They also realized that they were spending an inadequate amount of time with the 80% of the workforce that had the capability to be successful but were not exhibiting success on a consistent basis. As soon as the leaders refocused their energy, they began to see more results from their coaching efforts.

The biggest payback that you will have as a leader is in spending time with the 80%. Also, the exciting news is that most of these people can develop self-propelled characteristics. However, you must understand that there is "some assembly required." If you want most of your people to be self-propelled, you must take specific actions consistently until everyone believes they really are supposed to be self-propelled. Do not get frustrated because your people do not perform correctly the first time around. Just recognize that they need something different if they are going to develop the self-propelled characteristics you desire.

Action Steps

- Look at the list you developed at the end of Chapter One. What percentage of your people are demonstrating these behaviors on their own without having to be told to do so?

- What would be the benefit to you if most of your people were exhibiting the self-propelled characteristics that you identified at the end of the previous chapter? Economic benefit? Morale benefit?

- What are the obvious things that you need to change if you want your people to become self-propelled?

CHAPTER FOUR

The Performance Success Formula

Success is never complicated. (It is, however, demanding.)

Papa was a master mechanic and inventor. He was equally good at explaining things in a simple way that even a teenager could understand. The self-propelled mower was a series of gears with teeth and small chains that look like bicycle chains. When the self-propelled lever was pushing down, one of the gears that was connected to the motor hooked into one of the chains. This chain was connected to another gear that was connected to two of the wheels. When the chain began to move, off the lawnmower would go.

The performance success formula

If you want self-propelled people, it is essential that you understand what it takes to develop them. In this chapter we will take the cover off the gearbox, so to speak, so that you can understand the ingredients needed for someone to become self-propelled.

Helping your people achieve success is actually not complicated. It can be demanding but it is not complicated. There are five ingredients to developing a self-propelled person. If you are willing to invest the time and energy to help someone develop in each of these areas, you will quickly begin to see your people develop self-propelled characteristics. These five ingredients are found in the Performance Success Formula below:

Performance Coaching Principle #4

The Performance Success Formula
Goals + Skills + Knowledge + Beliefs +
Reinforcement = Performance Success

<u>Goals</u>

In order to develop self-propelled people, you must help them establish clear goals. While this may sound obvious, many leaders miss this simple and essential dimension of success. Without clear goals,
people do not know where to focus their energy and effort. Even with the best of intentions, they may be focusing their energy in the wrong place. There are two types of goals people must have if they are going to be successful. They must have *Performance goals* (measurable goals) and *Behavioral goals* (observable goals).

<u>Performance goals</u>

Performance goals are the measurable goals that the individual or team must achieve if they are going to be successful. The key to *Performance goals* is the word measurable. If they are not measurable, they are not performance goals. The following are examples of *Performance goals*:

- Increase one's loan portfolio by ten percent.
- Recommend three other bank products when opening a new account.
- Balance your teller drawer to within X dollars.

In some positions, performance may be more difficult to measure. Even in these positions, though, leaders should seek to define measurable goals that can help someone to track their performance.

Behavioral goals

Behavioral goals are the observable behaviors that someone must exhibit consistently if they are to achieve the *Performance goals*. These goals are usually not measurable in the traditional sense of that term. They are instead observable.

Tragically, most leaders do not develop *Behavioral goals* with their people. Usually *Behavioral goals* are not developed because leaders assume employees understand the expected behavior. Leaders believe that they should not have to be specific regarding behavior. Either way, not developing *Behavioral goals* is a bad leadership decision. Remember, 80% need guidance and coaching. Developing *Behavioral goals* is simply a tool to help in the coaching process.

The key to successful *Behavioral goals* is to define them in such a manner that they are "observable" to everyone in the same way. For example, initiative is one of the behaviors most leaders would like to see in their people. By itself, the term "initiative" is open to many different interpretations. The only way to escape this trap is to define what initiative looks like in this position. If you say, "Initiative means that when you are finished with your work, you check with others in the department to see if there is a way that you can assist them," then initiative takes on a more concrete meaning. Now, initiative is more observable. If you see someone sitting at his desk doing nothing while others around him are working feverishly, you have a more objective way to address the issue with the person. If you assume that your people "should" understand without defining behavioral goals, you make a big mistake. Define it and they will usually achieve it.

Skills

Having the necessary skills is the second element needed for performance success. Without proper skills, people will have difficulty achieving their goals. This is an area where many leaders make deadly assumptions. Too often leaders assume that someone possesses a certain set of skills when in fact they do not. There are four types of skills needed for someone to be successful: technical skills, problem-solving skills, time and task management skills, and relational skills.

Technical skills

Technical skills are the specific technical skills that employees must have to do their job. For a customer service representative it may be knowing how to access customer information. For a loan officer, it may be knowing how to follow good credit procedures. For someone in the operations area, it may be knowing how to use customized software.

Problem solving skills

Problem solving skills are the ability to use a logical process to identify and resolve problems. Many organizations expect their people to know how to do this when they hire them. Unfortunately, many people have never been taught how to effectively solve problems in a logical and orderly manner. This often results in frustration. "I thought surely that they knew how to solve problems" is a phrase expressed often by frustrated leaders.

Time and task management skills

An often-overlooked set of skills is time and task management skills. These are the skills necessary to organize and prioritize work in order for the most important work to be done in a timely manner. Leaders often assume that people know how to manage their time and tasks, when in reality they do not. This is particularly a temptation for leaders who are self-starters. Self-starters manage their time and task on their own. These self-starters often assume that everyone else does also. This is a costly assumption.

Relational skills

Relational skills refer to the skills needed to communicate, cooperate, resolve conflicts, and work effectively with co-workers, customers, and suppliers. Relational skills have traditionally been called the soft skills and are in contrast to technical skills, which have been called the hard skills. The irony is that people usually get in trouble because they lack soft skills, not because they lack hard skills. The biggest problem with referring to relational skills as "soft skills" is that the name itself implies that they are not as important as "hard skills." From a leadership perspective, if you see some skills as essential and others as "nice to have but not essential," your people will begin to treat them the same way. Sadly, this is what usually happens in organizations. A leader sends the message that certain skills are not essential, and the people therefore do not focus on those skills. Remember the 80%? They are going to deliver what they believe the leader really wants. The reality is that both sets of skills are essential even though they are different.

Knowledge

If you want your people to be self-propelled, they must be informed. People who are informed are more likely to be self-propelled than people who are uninformed. Knowledge and skills are very closely related but are slightly different. If someone possesses the skills to do something, they know how to do a procedure or process. They may know how to run a machine or fill out a form. Knowledge means that they not only can do the process but that they understand it. They can consider the implications of their actions on the rest of the process, and can solve problems related to the process. Knowledge is much broader than just knowing the skill. There are three types of knowledge that every person must possess if they are going to be successful: technical knowledge, relational knowledge and organizational knowledge.

Technical knowledge

Technical knowledge is the knowledge that someone must have if he is going to be successful at the technical part of his job. For example, a loan officer must know the technical steps to ensure that an applicant has good credit. The loan officer must also know the history of the individual and his or her potential for growth to determine if a loan should be given.

People need to have knowledge related to their roles, responsibilities and expectations. For example, I heard a senior vice president for loan production relate the following story. A teller was approached by someone to cash a check from a company that did business with the bank. The owner of the company had recently transferred some money into the company account but it had not appeared in the computer files. The teller denied the check. The employee was very embarrassed and upset. The owner was furious and took all of his business to another bank. If leaders want employees to succeed they must be sure the employees know the definition of success as well as their present position in relation to the goal.

Relational knowledge

To work cooperatively with others, people must possess a basic understanding of themselves and of others. They should be aware of how they react in different situations and also how their fellow team members react, as well as have a general understanding of what is important to their co-workers.

In addition to this, people also need a basic knowledge of what is expected in the organization regarding communication, cooperation and resolution of conflict. If expectations are clearly defined and communicated in these areas and if people are taught the skills to be successful in each area, the chances of success are greatly increased.

Organizational knowledge

There is another type of knowledge that is equally as important in today's team-based, customer-driven culture – organizational knowledge. The day of people coming to work and doing what they are told with little or no thought about why they are doing it is over. If people's actions affect the bottom line, they must know the impact of their behavior on the organization.

- Everyone needs to know where the organization is going. This means that everyone must understand what the mission, vision and values are for the organization.
- People also have to know the goals of the organization and how their jobs relate to these goals.
- People need to understand the culture of the organization and what really drives the organization. Everyone has observed someone "stick their foot in their mouth" because they did not understand the way the culture worked in an organization. It is important as a leader that you help your people understand really how the culture works.
- People need to have knowledge of the structure of the organization. If you want people to be self-propelled, they must know how the organization is structured and how different departments relate to each other. In seminars people commonly say that their people do not really understand how their actions affect others in the organization. If people do not understand the structure of the organization and how they relate to and affect each other, it is difficult for them to be successful.

Beliefs

Most training usually focuses on improving behavior. While behavior is important, what people believe is most important. Belief precedes behavior. People act the way they do because of what they believe. If people are going to achieve success, they must possess some essential beliefs about themselves, the organization, and their role in the organization. Here are a few of the essential beliefs that someone must have to achieve performance success:

Beliefs about self
- My success is my responsibility.
- I do possess the skills and knowledge to be successful.

- If I don't know what skill or knowledge is needed, my job is to ask.

Beliefs about the person's role in the organization
- How I work with others is as important as the technical part of my job.
- I am accountable to my peers.
- My job is to think and act based on what is in the best interest of the organization.
- What I do matters.

Beliefs about the organization
- The organization is committed to success.
- The organization cares about me.
- My leaders can be trusted.

This is only a partial list of the beliefs needed to be successful. Remember, the emphasis of this book is on helping the 80% who are adapters become self-propelled people. The self-starters are going to do the right thing regardless of what the organization says or does. You have little to worry about with the self-starters. Your concern as a coach should be with the 80% that have to be molded and coached. If they do not believe that the organization cares about them, they will have a tendency to invest less in their daily work and thereby harm the organization. If they do not believe in their own skills and abilities, they will be hesitant in their actions, thus lessening their effectiveness in the organization.

Reinforcement

The last part of the Performance Success Formula is reinforcement. While it is last in the equation, reinforcement may be the most important part of the equation. The 80% are going to respond based on the reinforcement they receive. They are heavily influenced by what the culture reinforces. Here is a simple example. Most leaders will say that the performance of their people is a key element in the success of their organization. How many times a year, though, does the leader review performance with the person? Many organizations are still in the pattern of only reviewing performance once a year unless someone makes a big mistake. If something is discussed only once a year, will someone think this is important? In most cases the answer is no. If the budget is reviewed on a monthly basis and performance is reviewed once a year, what is the obvious message that the people get?

There are three types of essential reinforcements if someone is going to be successful: structural reinforcement, resource reinforcement, and coaching reinforcement.

Structural Reinforcement

Structural Reinforcement refers to the systems, processes, procedures and structure that the organization uses to accomplish its goals. Does the organization have a clear plan for success? Are the systems and processes used to accomplish goals defined and monitored? Are the communication systems in the organization established so that everyone has the knowledge needed to be successful? Is there a clear problem solving system? Is there a system for people to make improvements or suggestions that will benefit the organization?

Resource Reinforcement

The next area of reinforcement is that of resources. Do the people in the organization have the people and material resources needed to do their job? While consulting with a client recently, I discovered that people in some of the departments were having difficulty getting supplies required for their job. The supplies were in the building, but people were having to stop and spend valuable minutes finding supplies that should have been at their work station. If you are expecting people to achieve certain performance levels, you must make sure they have the necessary resources, whether they are supplies, equipment, or people.

Coaching Reinforcement

Finally, there is coaching reinforcement. Coaching reinforcement means that leaders are effectively doing the things that are being advocated in this book to help their people be successful. Coaching reinforcement is the essence of this book.

Performance Success Formula Checklist

For your people to be successful, each part of the Performance Success Formula must be evaluated and developed in your organization. The following checklist can help you identify what has presently been done in your organization and what should be considered in the future.

Performance Success Formula checklist
- Have you developed *Performance goals* and *Behavioral goals* for each person in the organization?
- Have you identified the technical, problem solving, and relational skills essential for each person to be successful in his role?
- If people lack these skills, is there a training process in place for them to learn these skills?

- Have you identified the technical, relational, and organizational knowledge someone must possess to be successful in this position? If not, complete the following sentence: For someone to be successful in this position he must have this knowledge... Be as specific as possible.
- If people lack this knowledge, is there a training process in place for them to learn it?
- Have you identified essential beliefs for success in your organization?
- Have these been communicated with your people?
- Have all of the processes and systems used in your organization been clearly defined?
- Have you involved your staff in improving these systems?
- Do people have the needed material resources to achieve success?
- Does your organization have the needed people resources to achieve success?
- Do you have a defined process to give your people feedback on their performance?
- Do you have a defined process to coach your people to improve their performance?

Action Step

Review each of the items in the checklist. Develop strategies to address the items that you have not accomplished.

CHAPTER FIVE

Key Leadership Principles

Belief always precedes behavior.

Papa continued my education by talking about the key principles that I had to understand if I wanted to keep the lawnmower running at top efficiency. "John, a lawnmower is actually a simple machine. If you will keep oil in the lawnmower, keep the gears lubricated, keep the nuts and bolts tightened and clean grass from under the lawnmower, you will have a self-propelled lawnmower for a long time."

Leading people effectively is a little like Papa's talk with me. If you understand certain key principles, you can dramatically improve your effectiveness as a leader.

The four characteristics that your people need from you as a leader

Your people need four things from you if they are to become self-propelled. If you can provide these four things, you will see an immediate improvement in the productivity and morale of your people.

Clarity of Vision

The first thing they need is to know that you have a clear vision of where you are going, where the organization is going and how to get there. People get excited when they believe they are a part of something important. They get motivated when they are with leaders who are excited about the work they are doing. Here are some questions for you to ponder:

- Do you have a clear vision or goal for your organization?
- Is this your vision or is it just something that someone else said you should do?
- Is this vision contagious? Is it something that you are excited about and something that will excite others?
- Is the vision understood by your people? The vision is of no value if you do not share it with others.

Genuine Caring

This may be the most essential element of effective coaching. Do you really care about your people and their personal and professional growth? Most leaders will say, "Of course I care about my people." The question, though, begs that you go to a deeper level and ask another set of questions:

- Do you care enough about your people to learn what really motivates them?
- Do you care enough about your people to address problems when you see them?
- Do you care enough about your people to hold them accountable?
- What do you do on a daily basis that communicates to your

people that you genuinely care about them?

- What do you do on a daily, weekly or monthly basis that communicates to your people that you are concerned about their personal and professional growth?
- How do you get feedback from your people to insure that your actions are received as you intended?

Consistency of Action

The third thing that your people need from you is consistency of action. They need for you to be reasonably the same from day to day. Everyone will have problems from time to time. Even the best leaders will have days when they are not at their best. Are you reasonably the same, though, from day to day? Remember, the 80% that are the focus of this book rely on your reinforcement and coaching to achieve the level of performance that you desire. If you are not predictable, you are actually working counter to what you say you want to achieve.

Commitment to Persevere

The final thing that your people need from you is commitment to persevere until success is achieved. Are you willing to "stay the course" until success is achieved? Can you persevere during difficult times when it would be easy to give in? If you are willing to stay the course and be consistent with the vision that you espouse, you will soon discover that your people will begin exhibiting the characteristics that you desire.

Whether they are vice presidents looking to you as the president, CEO, or they are people looking to you as their first line supervisor, all people need to know that their leader has a vision for their organization and that they are working to achieve that vision.

You are responsible to your people, not for your people

"Big things often come in small packages." You have probably heard that phrase. For leaders, the following ten words can have profound impact. "You are responsible *to* your people, not *for* them." For some people this may be a subtle distinction, but for leaders it is a huge difference. Many leaders assume that they are responsible for their people's success. The only problem with this thought process is that you are to blame when they fail. In some cases (maybe even many cases) the leader may be a major part of the problem, but ultimately success is the responsibility of the person.

You, the leader, are responsible to your people. This means that you are responsible to do all of the things within your control to create an environment where they can be successful. This means that you are responsible for making sure that they are trained properly, that they are given good feedback and coaching, that problems are discussed when they arise, that they have the right resources to get the job done, and that the culture reinforces their success. There are, however, people in every field who are not successful even when the leader has done everything within his or her control. If as a leader you are doing everything within your control, you can then honestly say, "I have done everything within my control to help them be successful. This may not be the right job for this person." They either are not capable of doing the job, or they do not have the desire to achieve the level of success needed. If you believe that you are responsible to your people, you will do everything within your control to help them be successful, but you will recognize that their success is ultimately their own responsibility.

Realities of leading people today

What you believe about the world in which you live is just as important as what you believe about yourself and your role. Below are three realities about the workplace today that will impact your leadership ability.

- <u>People have different expectations of work today than in days past.</u>

Work is more than a paycheck for many people today. People want to be valued and appreciated. They want to believe that what they do on a daily basis is meaningful. Think about this for a moment. If the people in your organization stay with you until they retire, they will spend more time with you and the people in your organization than with the people, organizations, and things that they say are the most important things in their lives. If, as their leader, you work to make their work more enjoyable and productive, you will find that it not only enhances their work life, but also enhances their life outside of work.

- <u>Helping people improve their productivity is a major responsibility of leaders.</u>

Helping your people improve their performance is a major task of every leader. This has always been the case and always will be. This reality does not just apply in business and industry. Everyone from government to hospitals, non-profit organizations to education are trying to improve quality, productivity and customer service. In this workplace where so much emphasis is placed on high quality, quick response, customer service, and totally integrated organizational systems, the need for each member of the organization to achieve *performance goals* is critical. To a large degree your success as a leader will be measured by how well your people perform on a consistent basis. Getting results is still important- always has been, always will be. **The issue is not whether we get results, the issue is how we get results.**

That may sound rather cold and harsh, but it is not intended to be so.

It is actually intended to reflect reality. In any organization, whether it is a Fortune 500 company or a community bank, a leader who cannot aid an organization to achieve results in a desirable manner will soon be dismissed. Think about it for a moment. Why are leaders hired? Usually it is because someone believes he or she can help the organization improve. They usually say, "She is a great motivator. She knows how to get the most out of her people. She will improve the bottom line." All of these comments are about performance.

- <u>Your relationship with your direct reports is the most important relationship in your organization</u>.

Whether you are the president of the organization, the credit manager or a branch manager, your relationship with your direct reports is the most critical relationship in your organization. Most people develop their view of the organization based on how they relate to their direct contact leader. If you are creating an environment where they feel valued and appreciated, they will usually respond positively to your leadership. If you create the expectation that you want them to be self-propelled and then reinforce it with your actions, 80% of your people will become the self-propelled person you desire.

Belief precedes behavior

Performance Coaching Principle #5

Belief precedes behavior.

Most leaders focus on what their people do and then seek to correct problem behavior. While this approach will lead to partial success, it will not help you achieve the level of success that you desire. If you want to develop self-propelled people, you must understand that behavior will only change permanently when people change the beliefs that drive the behavior. This is truly a revolutionary part of this performance coaching process. Belief always precedes behavior. Stop focusing on what people are doing and focus on why they are doing it. This is the only way to correct problem behavior.

If people are going to act differently, they must first think differently. While this is rather obvious, it is an area that few leaders are willing to explore. Most leaders are just concerned with people acting right, without realizing that the person without the right mindset will not be able to sustain correction action.

If a leader really believes that his job is to "control" and tell people what to do, his actions will naturally follow in this manner. He may be able to modify these patterns for a period of time, but he will not be able to sustain the changed behavior because he has not changed his foundational beliefs.

A few years ago I was leading a performance coaching workshop at an organization in the Southeast. All morning the participants had been addressing the importance of developing a coaching mindset and the corresponding set of beliefs about their roles and responsibilities. More than once, I had said, "As a coach, you must help your people learn to think like a self-propelled person. There is no need for you as a leader to yell, cuss or get aggressive with your people. If you are helping them develop the right beliefs and holding them accountable for their behavior, you will find your job as a coach much easier, more enjoyable and more successful." About halfway through the afternoon, one young man raised his hand to ask a question. He was a bright young manager in his early thirties. "John, I understand all of this nice stuff about coaching your people. At what point, though, do you decide that it is time to get tough and "kick butt?"

These simple words testify that this young leader really did not understand the coaching mindset. As a coach, there is no need to "kick butt" with your people. This type of power and intimidation does not produce self-propelled people. It leads to compliant and submissive people, not self-confident and thinking people who can take appropriate action without having to be closely watched every day.

What you believe is far more important than what you do. Change your beliefs and you will change your leadership style.

Understand the change factors

As you make changes in your life and as you help your people change, you must understand the change process. For change to occur, the person making the change must move through four essential steps:

Catalyst - First, something must cause you to stop and look. This is called a catalyst. A catalyst may be self-originating or it may be someone or something external. For example, if someone is to stop smoking, something must cause him to stop and look at his behavior. This something may be an inner awareness that smoking is not good for him and will shorten his life. It may also be a physical problem related to smoking. An example of an external cause is a spouse or child who urges him to quit. It may be a physician who tells him that he will die an early death if he continues. Whatever the source of the catalyst, he will not stop smoking until something causes him to stop and look at his existing behavior.

Awareness – The awareness step is the time when you actually stop and look. Some people are presented with a catalyst yet they refuse to stop and look at their behavior. These people really have no desire to change their behavior.

Comprehension – The comprehension step is that moment when we understand the impact of our existing actions. In the awareness step we see it. In the comprehension step we understand the impact of our actions.

Conviction – For change to really take place, the person must move to the final step: Conviction. Conviction is an internal belief that you must change your behavior. It is an inner awareness that the existing behavior is not helping you achieve what you desire. For conviction to transform into changed behavior, it must be accompanied by commitment. Commitment is the action that comes from the belief of conviction.

When I was a pastor, there was a middle-aged man in the church who had been a heavy smoker since his teenage years. His physician discovered cancer in one of his lungs and removed it. Fortunately, all of the cancer was removed. When he was still in the hospital his physician told him, "You must quit smoking now. If you do not, it will kill you!"

A few weeks after he left the hospital, I went to a meeting in another town. My route took me past his house. I stared in amazement as I saw him standing in his front yard smoking. Regardless of what the physician said, he was not convicted to change his behavior.

Action Steps

Reserve approximately one hour that you can be undisturbed. Make an honest assessment of your beliefs. Identify which beliefs are empowering you to move forward in making change. Identify the beliefs that are holding you back from making change.

This brings the first section of "Self-Propelled People" to a close. The second section explores the Performance Coaching process in detail.

Section I
Performance Coaching   Principles

Performance Coaching Principle #1
To develop self-propelled people you must have a clear understanding of what a self-propelled person looks and acts like.

Performance Coaching Principle #2
If you want people to become self-propelled,
you have to do something different.

Performance Coaching Principle #3
The 10/80/10 Principle – In an average group of people, approximately 10% come pre-assembled with all of the skills, knowledge and characteristics desired. Eighty percent (80%) are adapters who possess part of the skills, knowledge and characteristics and need some assembly.   Ten percent (10%) are "unassemblable" (They are not going to be successful regardless of what you do).

Performance Coaching Principle #4
The Performance Success Formula
Goals + Skills + Knowledge + Beliefs +
Reinforcement = Performance Success

Performance Coaching Principle #5
Belief precedes behavior.

Section II

The Performance Coaching Process

Developing self-propelled people requires more than the right mindset and the right skills. The other key to developing self-propelled people is having a defined process that you use to coach and develop your people. This section will detail a process that you can use to turn your people into self-propelled people. If you already have a performance evaluation process in place, you can adapt this process very easily to your existing process.

(In this section dialogue with staff may be demonstrated. When this occurs, the dialogue will be in italics.)

CHAPTER SIX

The Performance Coaching Process, an Overview

Regular feedback is the key to long-term success.

Every leader wants successful people in his or her organization. Unfortunately, most people don't come with everything they need to be successful. If your people don't have the desired skills, knowledge and beliefs, then you or someone will have to teach them and coach them until they develop them. This is where the "wheels come off" for many leaders. Most leaders do not understand the mechanics of coaching.

Whether you are coaching individuals or teams, the steps in the coaching process are the same. This chapter will provide a general overview of the process. The details of each step in the coaching process will be examined in detail in the following chapters.

Performance coaching principle #6

Regular feedback is the key to long-term success.

There are four steps in the performance coaching process:

- The Goal step   Establishing goals and expectations
- The Observation step   Observing behavior
- The Awareness step   Discussing performance
- The Alignment step   Correcting performance problems

<u>*Step One – The goal step*</u>

The first step in performance coaching is to clearly define the goals and expectations for the person or team. These should be defined in a way that enables the person to have a clear understanding of these goals and expectations. There are two types of goals that should be established – *Performance goals* and *Behavioral goals*.

- *Performance goals* are the measurable goals that the person must achieve to be successful in his position.

- *Behavioral goals* are the observable behaviors that one must exhibit if he is to be successful at his *Performance goals*. Most leaders never really define *Behavioral goals* with their people. This is tragic because behavioral goals are the key to developing self-propelled people. *Behavioral goals* must be established in a way that makes them objective so that all parties are seeing the expected behaviors in the same way.

Step Two – The observation step

Once the goals have been clearly defined, understood and agreed upon, the coach must develop a plan to observe the behaviors and performance of the person or team. Observing behavior is the only way to know if someone is achieving goals in the right way. Performance is observed in the following four ways:

- Physically observing the person's performance.
- Reviewing data related to performance.
- Receiving feedback from others inside the organization, as well as customers and suppliers.
- Having the person assess his or her own performance.

Step Three – The awareness step

Once behavior has been observed, the next step is to discuss this behavior with the individual or team. If the behavior is correct, positive performance should be reviewed and praised to reinforce the right behavior. If there are problems with performance, the leader should plan a caring strategy to help the person examine the problem behavior.

Step Four – The alignment step

If there are problems with performance, the correct behavior should be defined and agreed upon. This is the essence of the alignment step. As a part of correcting performance problems, the coach should establish a follow-up plan to ensure that the right behavior is achieved. In the following chapters, each step in the process will be reviewed in detail.

The importance of feedback

Accurate, effective, and ongoing feedback is central to developing self-propelled people. Each of the three adjectives in the previous sentence was chosen intentionally.

- Feedback must be accurate. This means that you must first observe your people so that you know what their performance really is. Accurate feedback is the only way to help people grow.

- The feedback must also be effective. "Effective" in this case indicates that "how you provide the feedback" enables the person to really understand her performance. Many people give feedback, but do so in a way that creates more problems than solutions.

- Ongoing is the final term. Feedback must be ongoing if it is to be truly useful. Therefore, you must give your people feedback numerous times during the year.

The two biggest mistakes that leaders make

The coaching mistakes that leaders make usually occur because their feedback is not accurate, effective or ongoing. There are two major mistakes that leaders make in coaching their people.

- The first mistake is only evaluating people once a year. Remember the 80%. They are going to do what you reinforce. If you talk about goals once a year and then do not talk about goals again for a full year, the person will not think that goals are really important. In addition, the person may think that he is doing fine because you are not talking with him about his performance when in fact he may not be meeting expectations.

- The second mistake is to make the evaluation of performance subjective. This is the biggest problem with most performance coaching. In far too many cases, the evaluation of the person's performance is very subjective. The leader thinks that the person is not performing up to the appropriate level. The person thinks he or she is doing acceptable performance. In these situations, it becomes the leaders opinion versus the person's opinion. The way to resolve this is to be sure that *Performance goals* are measurable and to define *Behavioral goals* in a way that you and the person have a clear understanding of what the behavior looks like.

Coaching on a yearly basis

Providing feedback for people on a regular basis is an essential part of developing self-propelled people. To do this there must be a defined process to give feedback throughout the year. There are three parts to a total coaching system: the annual performance coaching session; formal follow-up coaching sessions; and spontaneous coaching sessions.

The annual performance coaching session

This session is the initial coaching session that you will have with your people each year. This annual session should be one-fourth review of last year's performance and three-fourths coaching and establishing new goals for the next year. The focus of the session is to look forward, developing strategies for the coming year. If you are coaching throughout the year, the person is aware of his or her performance by the time the annual session occurs. (See *Note* on page 68.)

There are five steps you should complete during the annual coaching session:

- Assess the present level of performance.
- Celebrate area where the performance meets or exceeds expectations.
- Clearly define *Behavioral goals* and *Performance goals* for the coming year.
- Develop strategies with the person to improve his performance in areas that need to be improved.
- Develop a follow-up plan to track progress during the coming twelve months. The length of the meeting is usually from one to three hours with each person. This will vary depending on the level of coaching needed with the individual.

Preparation for the annual coaching session

The following checklist can assist you as you prepare for the annual coaching session:

- Set the time for the session well in advance so the person is not caught off-guard.
- Have the person reflect on his own performance during the past year before he comes to the meeting. You may even have him identify areas where you think he has excelled and where he needs to improve. Some leaders have the person even fill out an evaluation form on himself.
- Provide privacy with a minimum of interruptions.
- Know what you want to accomplish during the meeting.
- Plan for the conversation using the dialogue-planning tree (Chapter Sixteen). Consider the person's point of view when you plan the conversation. Have your opening comments prepared.

- Have the necessary forms and factual information in front of you.
- Be sure that the person has identified goals that he wants to accomplish during the coming year.
- Plan your follow-up before you begin the meeting.
- Make sure that your focus is on helping the person be successful.

One final note about the annual coaching session. It is important that you end the annual coaching session in the following way. First, summarize the discussion and review any decisions that have been made. Next, communicate to the person that you want him to be successful. Let him know that the coaching sessions during the coming year are a part of helping him be successful.

Formal follow-up coaching sessions (quarterly or semiannually)

The second step of the coaching process is the formal follow-up sessions. The purpose of these meetings is to make sure the person is on track with the established goals from the annual session. If there are problems, this allows for "mid course correction" that can quickly get the person back on track to achieve his desired goals. There should be a minimum of one of these formal follow-up sessions during the year. For best results, they should be done quarterly.

The formal follow-up session is a great opportunity for you to help your people stay on track toward their goals. This follow-up session is also a great way for you to build a strong relationship with your people. Unfortunately, the lack of formal follow-up sessions is the greatest mistake that leaders make. If your people know that these sessions are going to occur, they will be more conscious of their behavior and their performance. Remember the 80% of your people that are adapters. They will perform according to what you reinforce.

Many leaders do not believe they have time to do quarterly follow-ups each year, especially if they take from one to three hours. The follow-up meetings, however, are not intended to be long. If the performance of the person is on track, these meetings can be done in fifteen to thirty minutes. This short meeting can also be a great opportunity for you to praise people for positive performance.

Spontaneous coaching

In the course of daily work, there will be times when you will observe behaviors that should be praised and behavior that needs to be improved. These are the times when you must do immediate performance coaching. The details of how to do the daily performance coaching are found in Chapters Eighteen, Nineteen and Twenty. Here are a couple of thoughts that can help you with daily coaching:

- When you see something done right, immediately praise and identify the correct behavior to reinforce it in the person's mind.
- When you see problem behavior, immediately (or as quickly as possible) meet with the person to discuss the problem behavior.

Recording performance during the year

One of the important coaching tasks is providing accurate feedback. To do this you must keep accurate records during the year. This is often a problem for many leaders. They do not have an effective system for recording the behavior of people. As a result, leaders often only record the problems people have. This leads to a very unbalanced perspective on the person.

There are some very simple ways that you can eliminate this problem and provide accurate feedback for your people year round. Here are two options:

- If you do not have a method for recording comments try this simple system. Get a calendar for each person that you lead. Every two to four weeks write down your observations about their performance. If a noteworthy event, either positive or negative happens during the month, immediately write it down when it occurs. If there is a problem that occurs and the person corrects the problem, note both the problem and also the fact that the person corrected the action. When review time comes, you will then have a balanced review of performance during the entire year with both positive and negative comments.

- Another method is to develop a manila folder for each person. Once a month or more frequently take a "sticky note" and write down your observations for the person that month. Put the "sticky note" in the folder and move to the next person's folder. When a noteworthy event occurs during the month, write it on a "sticky note" and put it in the folder.

Do not worry about semantics

You can call this process whatever you want. The following are some of the names that people use to define the process: performance coaching sessions, success reviews, performance reviews, performance assessment, and yearly goal setting meetings. The words used to describe the process are not as important as what you do in the process. Follow-up and your commitment to the process are the essential elements to success.

Distinguishing between levels of performance

After reviewing many performance review forms, I have found a wide variety of methods for differentiating levels of performance. The problem with most of these forms is that they are subjective in how performance is reviewed. For example, many forms have a 1-5 scale or 1-10 scale evaluating the person. When leaders are asked to define the difference between the five levels, however, they struggle with defining what constitutes the difference between a three and a four or a four and a five. When using a rating system, you must clearly and objectively define the behavior for each rating. If this cannot be done, performance evaluation remains subjective.

Most people's performance falls into one of three categories. If you do not already have a defined process to distinguish between levels of performance, consider the following thoughts:

Distinguished or Superior – This is the person who goes substantially beyond what is expected in the job. This category is usually reserved for those whose performance is obviously distinguished from those who meet the expectations of the job. Most likely, the only persons who will fall into this category are those who are in the ten percent –the "pre-assembled" category of the 10/80/10 principle.

Successful – This is the rating for those that meet the expectations of the job. This will be the majority of the persons working for you. These individuals are doing exactly what you ask them to do in their role.

Needs improvement – This rating is given when someone is not meeting expectations of the job. The performance is unacceptable and below minimum standards.

Closing Thoughts

Whatever process you use for evaluating performance, it is important that you evaluate performance in an accurate, effective and ongoing manner. If you will do these three things, you will see the performance levels of your people improve.

Action Step

If you have not already established *Performance goals* and *Behavioral goals* for your people, develop them during the next sixty days.

Note: TIP - Technology Improving Performance is the easiest and most effective performance appraisal and review tool available on the market. I would highly recommend the TIP performance appraisal and review software for every organization. Visit them online at www.tipsoftware.com to watch a FREE guided demo of the software and see just how TIP can help your organization. JTB

CHAPTER SEVEN

The Goal Step
Defining Goals and Expectations

If your people know where to go and how to get there, it is much easier for them to be successful.

(In Chapters Seven through Eleven, we will use an ongoing story of a woman named Susan to illustrate the coaching process.) Susan is a new person in your organization. She is bright and energetic. She appears to have many of the skills and attributes that you seek in your organization. You want to start her career in a positive and proactive way by clearly defining goals and expectations. You are presently entering the goal step of performance coaching.

Performance Coaching Principle #7

Success requires clearly defined goals and expectations.

Susan's success in your organization will be based on a combination of factors. Some of those factors are within Susan's control: her attitude, her willingness to learn, and her persistence. Some of them are within your control: the work culture, good work systems, clearly defined goals, and strategies to achieve goals. As Susan's leader, you must remember that your primary objective is to help her move toward success by providing the items within your control. Creating an environment where your people can be successful is your primary job as a leader. Unfortunately, it is easy to let your other responsibilities get in the way of your primary job. One part of helping your people become successful is helping them develop clear goals and strategies to achieve these goals.

Establishing goals is the initial step of the performance coaching process. There are five actions to be accomplished during the goal step:

- Define the Performance goals if they are not already established.
- Define the behaviors needed to be successful in a way that is clearly understood and agreed upon by you and the person or team. These are called Behavioral goals.
- Establish a plan to develop the beliefs, knowledge and skills necessary to achieve the Performance goals and Behavioral goals.
- Develop a time line for learning the new behaviors and skills.
- Establish follow-up plans to track the progress of the individual or team.

It is important that the leader and the individual or group leave the goal step meeting with a clear understanding of the goals to be accomplished. It is not enough for the leader to assume that the people know what the goal is. You must use the questioning process (Chapter Sixteen) and listen effectively (Chapter Fifteen) to be certain that you and the other person have the same understanding in relation to the goals. You must develop the habit of saying, "Let's discuss specifically what this behavior looks like, because it is important that you be able to recognize successful behavior when you do it." Remember only 10% of the people in most organizations are going to do this on their own. To help the 80% be successful, the leader must clearly define behavior in a way that is observable by all.

If you have a regular performance review process in your organization, the goal step will occur during the annual review. If you do not have an annual review process, Chapter Six can show you how to develop one.

Establishing Performance Goals

When most people think of goals, they think of what we call *Performance goals*. *Performance goals* are the measurable goals that the person must achieve if he is going to be successful. *Performance goals* have the following characteristics:

- They must be measurable in some way –quantity, quality, percentages, efficiencies or other measurements.
- They should be directly related to the *Performance goals* of the organization.
- They should cause the person or team to stretch or grow in their professional career.
- These *Performance goals* should be developed in collaboration with the individual or team member whenever possible. There will be times when goals are established for your people by the organization. Even in these cases, though, the person should have some input into at least the implementation of the goals. Remember, if you desire to develop self-propelled people, they must learn how to set and achieve goals themselves. They will also "buy into" goals more when they have some input into setting the goals. The following steps can give you a strategy for helping your people set and achieve goals.

- Step One
  Define the goal to be set.
  Identify the specific areas where goals need to be set. Goals should be set in the areas that have the greatest impact on the success of the person and the organization.

- Step Two
  Discuss why the goal is important.
  Ask the following questions to the group:
  Why should we set a goal in this area?
  How will achieving a goal in this area benefit you and the organization?
  What will happen if the goal is achieved?
  What will happen if the goal is not achieved?

- Step Three
  Discuss how people feel or think about setting the goal.
  Ask what they feel or think about setting a goal in this area.

- Step Four
  Make your personal commitments to the person or team.
  You must commit to help them do the following:

  > Track their goal.
  > Develop strategies to achieve the goal.
  > Address issues that are outside of their control.

- Step Five
  Define the criteria for setting the goal.
  The criteria are really boundaries within which they should make their decisions. There are two type of criteria: essential and desirable.
  Essential criteria are things that must be included in their goals. These could mean that their average must be above a certain number.
  Desirable criteria are the things that would be nice in their goal but are not essential.

- Step Six
  Evaluate the goal options.
  Look at each of the suggested goals the person may discuss, evaluating them based on essential and desirable criteria.

- Step Seven
  Set the goal.
  You and the person agree on a goal.

- Step Eight
  Get everyone to commit to achieve the goal.
  Once the goal is set, you and the person(s) must make a personal commitment to achieve the goal.

- Step Nine
  Develop strategies to achieve the goal.
  Are there skills or knowledge that the person should develop?
  Are there resources that he or she needs to be successful?
  Does the person have a system in place to achieve the goal?
  Does the person have a communication plan related to this goal?
  Does the person have a plan to anticipate and solve problems that may arise?

Establishing Behavioral goals

Establishing *Performance goals* is only half of the goal setting process. It is actually the easy part. *Performance goals* are measurable. You either achieve them or you do not achieve them. It is more difficult and problematic for most leaders to assess behavior. Behavior, though, is critical to assess because behavior leads to performance success. The key to successfully assessing behavior is learning how to define behavior in a way that clearly explains what is expected.

Behavioral goals are the observable behaviors that the person or team must exhibit if they are to accomplish the *Performance goals* and be successful. The *Behavioral goals* refer to how the *Performance goals* are to be achieved. These will usually be observable rather than easily measured, although some may be measurable. These should be described in such a way that the leader and the person understand them the same way.

A simple example may help. Cooperation and teamwork are one of the behaviors expected of customer service representatives in organizations. Most leaders do not define exactly what they mean by teamwork and cooperation. As a result, what the leader is expecting and what the customer service representative means by cooperation may be entirely different. To get around this problem, the leader must say, "Cooperation and teamwork are essential behaviors to be successful in this job. Let's define what cooperation looks like so that you have a clear understanding of what is expected."

There are four steps to establishing *Behavioral goals:*

- Step One
  Review *Performance goals*. Review the *Performance goals* and identify the behaviors that someone must exhibit if they are going to achieve these *Performance goals*.

- Step Two
  Select Behavioral Categories - Select three to five of the categories identified below that describe the behaviors you identified in step one:

      Problem Solving
      Creativity
      Attention to Detail
      Customer Response
      Flexibility
      Initiative

Cooperation and Teamwork
Effective Communication
Planning and Organizing

These behaviors will usually fall into one of the categories listed above. By no means is this a definitive list. You may find other categories that you want to add to this list.

- Step Three
  Define the Behavior that describes each category selected in Step Two. You and the per son or team together answer the following question for each category selected in Step Two: What is the behavior that we should see if someone in this position is exhibiting this behavior? Continue defining each word until you have a clear, objective understanding of the behavior that is needed to be successful.

- Step Four
  Commit to achieve the Behavior Goal. Once the behavior has been defined, the leader and the person or team must make a personal commitment to achieve this behavior.

Some additional thoughts on Behavioral goals

- Why only three to five categories? Some people have asked, "Why only list three to five categories? All of these categories are important. Shouldn't we establish goals in each of these areas?" In an ideal world the answer might be yes. In the real world, though, if you establish Behavioral goals in all eleven categories listed above, people will generally feel a "system overload." Most people can only focus on a few areas at one time. The intent of focusing on three to five categories is to provide people a clear understanding of the most important factors for success.

- Step three is the most critical. Step three, defining the behavior, is the most critical part of the process. Without step three, behavior is still subjective and open to interpretation. It is "my opinion against your opinion." With step three, behavior becomes objective. When you and the person agree on a definition which both of you can understand; much of the subjectivity is removed. *"Susan, initiative is one of the behaviors that we expect from someone in this position. Let's define what initiative looks like so that we both know what we are looking for. What is the behavior, if you see it, that will tell you that someone is taking initiative?"* Let the person answer the question. Affirm the responses that are consistent with what you are seeking. If you do not understand a response, explore what the person means. If there are descriptors that need to be added to the definition of initiative, do so. It can be done in the following manner: *"Susan, I think these behaviors do describe part of what we are seeking in initiative. I also want to add these expectations related to initiative."*

- Planning for *Behavioral goals*
  It is important in the planing stage to identify the areas where behavioral expectations should be developed. Below are some thoughts on times or places where *Behavioral goals* should be defined.
  - Critical times of the day, week or month. These are the most important times that determine the success of the organization.
  - Critical contacts. These are the times where you make an impression with internal and external customers.
  - Cooperation between departments and groups.

- Be specific
  Remember, only about ten percent of the people in the work place have all of the characteristics, skills and knowledge that

you desire. The other ninety percent are going to wait and see where the organization is going before they commit to certain actions. These people will need specific expectations if they are going to achieve the desired level of performance.

Two useful coaching techniques

Two coaching techniques may be helpful during the Goal Step of the Performance Coaching process.

- Developing a learning plan
  The coaching process at some point will require the individual to learn and use a new set of skills or knowledge. To facilitate learning, a learning plan should be developed. The following are the steps to develop a learning plan so that the person's performance can improve.
    - Develop a list of the technical skills and the relationship or people skills that someone must possess to be successful in this role.
    - Identify the knowledge that the person must possess to do this job successfully.
    - Identify the training or experiences necessary for the person to obtain this knowledge or develop these skills.
    - Develop the criteria you must see before you are confident that the person has the needed knowledge or skills.
    - Develop an action plan to obtain the knowledge or skill, including a time line.
    - Develop a follow-up plan to help the per son monitor his or her growth.

- LPA
  Many people have difficulty learning more than one skill at a time. With this in mind it is helpful to use the LPA approach. LPA is an acronym for the three parts of the learning process:

Learn one skill at a time.

Practice the skill until you are confident in the person's ability to use the skill in a "real world" situation.

Apply the skill in a "real world" situation. Once you have seen the person use the skills in a real setting, evaluate the results and make adjustments so the person knows what the skill looks like and how to apply it successfully.

How to lead the goal step meeting

There are twelve steps in the Goal Step meeting.

- Step One - Explain the Performance Coaching Process -
  In this step you should help the person understand the importance of tracking and improving performance throughout the entire year.

- Step Two - Establish Ground Rules -
  Ground rules are the guidelines that you and the person or team use to guide your discussion and keep it focused on helping them be successful. Below are four examples of ground rules that we use in coaching sessions.
  - In discussions there are no right or wrong answers, just different perceptions.
    Discussion should consist of talking and listening, not arguing.
  - Focus on solutions to problems instead of people to blame. The emphasis is to avoid blaming and to seek solutions to problems. This ground rule is designed to eliminate the need for defensiveness and to focus on "how to get better."
  - Focus on things within your control.
    Emphasize to the person that the key to success is focusing on what is within his control. There will be a tendency for some people to focus on things outside of their control and

blame these for a lack of success. Help them understand that they must learn how to focus on the things that are within their control.

– When there is a request for commitment, take it seriously. Help the person understand that you are serious when you ask for his or her commitment to certain goals or behaviors.

- Step Three - Define the purpose and goals of this meeting-
Clarify why this meeting is taking place and what you want to accomplish in the meeting. *"Susan, the purpose of this meeting is for us to review your accomplishments during the past year and to establish and commit to goals for the coming year."*

- Step Four -Define *Performance* and *Behavioral goals*-
Make sure that you do this in collaboration with the other person. If certain goals already have been set for the person or team, communicate these. If there are no preset goals, then use the goal setting process described earlier in the chapter. When developing *Performance goals*, encourage the person to stretch, rather than just stay with a safe goal. It is also important to clearly identify what is negotiable and what is non-negotiable.

- Step Five - Identify beliefs, skills and knowledge needed -
Once goals are set, then you and the person must identify the skills, knowledge and beliefs needed to achieve these goals. Once these are listed, help the person identify which skills, knowledge and beliefs he already has and which ones he must learn.

- Step Six - Discuss why the goals are needed -
It is important that you and the person discuss why these goals are needed. If the person cannot identify why the goal is important, use the questioning process to examine why they cannot see the importance of this goal.

- Step Seven - Discuss how the goals are similar/different than the previous goals -
  Identifying how the new goal(s) is like existing goals or expectations will help many people begin to adapt to the goal. This step helps the person become more comfortable with the goal. If the goal is similar to what has been done in the past, the person will have confidence in his ability to achieve the goal (provided of course that he has met similar goals in the past). If the goal is different than goals in the past, it will give you an opportunity to help the person develop a strategy to be successful in the future. In this step use the questioning process often.

- Step Eight - Do a benefit analysis -
  For people to accept a goal they must see how the goal is going to help them. Use the questioning process to help the person define the benefit of achieving the new goal(s).

- Step Nine - Discuss how the person "feels or thinks" about the new behavior -
  Remember Performance Coaching Principle # 5, Belief always precedes behavior. If people do not believe in the goal or believe that the goal is achievable, they will not commit to achieve the goal. It is important that you ask questions to understand the thought process and the commitment to the goal.

- Step Ten - Get commitment to achieve the new goals -
  You must ask the person for commitment to achieve the goals and the person must say yes.

- Step Eleven - Develop an action plan and timeline to achieve the goals -
  Once there is commitment to the goal, an action plan must be developed to achieve the goal. It is important to include in the action plan any training or coaching that will be needed and a timeline for achieving the goal.

- Step Twelve - Develop a follow-up plan -
Before you leave the meeting, establish a follow-up plan so that
the person knows you will be working with them.

Action Step

Plan for and implement the goal step with at least one person in your
organization.

CHAPTER EIGHT

The Observation Step
Observing Behavior

The most obvious things are often the easiest to overlook.

Susan responded to the goal step very positively. She left with a clear understanding of what was expected and strategies to help her develop new skills. As her coach, your next step is to observe her so that you can give her good feedback on her performance. You are entering the observation step of the coaching process.

Performance Coaching Principle #8

To give accurate feedback on performance you must observe your people.

Once you have completed the goal step, your next strategy is to observe your people so that you can give them accurate feedback on their performance. It is essential that you develop a strategy to do this. If you do not develop an intentional strategy to observe your people, you will not get an accurate picture of their performance. You will then evaluate them based on isolated situations rather than a comprehensive observation of their performance.

General Guidelines for Observing People

While you can observe at any time, here are some general thoughts that will help you to observe natural behavior:

- Know the behavior you wish to observe. It is important to have a clear understanding of what to observe about people's behavior. Without this clear understanding, you may miss important behaviors or words that can help people succeed. It may be useful to review Chapter Fourteen, Breakdown Analysis, to help you identify what you specifically need to observe.

- Identify the times when you will most likely observe the behaviors that are defined in the *Behavioral goals*. You should also observe your people when they are in situations where problem behavior will potentially be demonstrated.

- Vary the times that you observe your people. There are some people who recognize your patterns and will modify their performance when you are present.

- Observe your people on a regular basis so that they are not anxious when you are present. If they only see you when there are problems, they will get anxious every time you come into the work area. You will not get an accurate reflection of their performance.

Preparation for Observing

- Prepare yourself emotionally - To effectively coach others, you must be prepared emotionally, mentally and physically. Here are some thoughts that can help you as you prepare for the observation phase:

  Clear your mind - To be effective as a coach, you must be able to focus on people and their performance. If things distract you mentally or emotionally, you may not see little behaviors that should be discussed.

  Have enough rest - The coaching process requires that you be on your toes. If you are tired, you will not be fresh and focused. This again may keep you from seeing certain behaviors that should be discussed.

  Know your emotional hooks - Each person has actions which "hook" them. These are the behaviors of others which cause you to lose focus.

  Remember your goal - Your real goal in the coaching process is to help people examine their thought process and behavior so that they can be successful in the future. You are on "their side."

  Anticipate scenarios - As a coach, you know that there may be confrontation. Anticipating these situations will help you prepare for the real situation.

  Recognize your biases toward the person - Do you have any biases toward the person or team? It is important that you recognize these. If you have a predisposition to believe certain things about a person, whether good or bad, you may inadvertently overlook topics, which should be included in your discussion.

  Plan the conversation - The introduction is perhaps the most critical part of the meeting. If you begin the meeting in a positive clear way, it will set a tone for the whole meeting. You should also use the dialogue-planning tree to anticipate potential problems that might occur in the conversation and how to manage these (Chapter Sixteen). Finally, you should plan the conclusion of the meeting and the follow-up.

How to Observe

There are four basic ways that you can observe your people and their performance:

- Actual observation of behavior-
  The most obvious way to observe performance is to be with your people and see it for yourself. When you are with your people, keep your eyes and ears open for behavior that you wish to discuss. When you see behavior that you want to discuss, do so as quickly as possible after the incident.

- Review written documentation related to performance-
  Written documentation related to performance may include reports or papers generated by the person or it may be a record of his efficiencies or effectiveness. Written documentation can often reveal patterns and trends that you may not see by simply observing someone's performance.

- Feedback from others-
  Feedback from others includes any feedback you receive from people in your organization or from people outside of your organization regarding this person. For example, another department in your organization may provide feedback on the accuracy of the person or the quality of his work. A customer outside of your organization may provide feedback on the quality of the service they receive. Also, if your organization provides a peer feedback process or a "360 degree" feedback process, this information can be very useful. A "360 degree" feedback process is a process where someone is evaluated by his leader, a selected number of his peers and some of his direct reports.

- Self-reflection by the person or team-
  The person may also give his personal assessment of his progress. Self-reflection can be a useful tool as it gives you a gauge to compare how you see his performance and how he sees his performance.

How to be objective when observing people

When you are observing people, remain as objective as possible. Being objective includes two parts:

First, being objective means that you cannot base your own self-worth on the other person's actions. If you can do this, you can see their actions for what they are, not what you want them to be. Basing your own self worth on other's actions hinders you from viewing their actions objectively.

Second, being objective means that you try not to put your own biases on their performance. Being objective will allow you to really see what is happening and then use the questioning process to discuss what you have observed.

Here are some simple actions that can help you remain objective when observing your people:

- Prepare yourself-
  Make sure that you avoid getting "hooked" emotionally when observing your people. When you get hooked, you may miss things that the person says or does or you may focus excessive attention on certain things that are not central to his performance.

- Define the times and best ways to observe their behavior.

- Identify the goal(s) or the things you want to specifically observe during your observation time.

- Communicate with your people about what you are doing.

- If you see behavior that meets or exceeds your expectations, praise people for it.

- If you see behavior that you do not understand, address it with them at the appropriate time (as soon as possible). Use the questioning approach. *"Susan, I saw you do this. Help me understand why you did that. What was your objective in doing that?"*

What to observe

When observing people, the first and most obvious thing you must know is exactly what to observe. If you do not know what to observe, you may miss very important actions that can tell you how people need to improve. The breakdown analysis that is described in Chapter Fourteen can assist you in defining the exact behavior that you should be observing. Here are some general guidelines for observing people.

- Observe at the "Macro" and "Micro" level.

  - Macro Level – The macro level means that you are looking at the "big picture." When you observe on the macro, you are watching the general flow of conversations and the way in which someone goes about doing his task. On the macro level you are looking for any patterns that should be explored that may give insight into why someone is successful or not successful.

– Micro Level – The micro level means that you are looking at the details of what the person does. The micro level looks at the specific words that someone says or actions that someone takes at a given moment. At the micro level, you may observe that a word choice seems odd or that a behavior seems unusual in a given situation. The micro level is designed to get below the surface to explore the underlying thought patterns or beliefs that produce a certain behavior.

When observing at the Micro level there are four basic actions to observe.

Observe what people say.
When observing what people say, the coach is listening for the words that people use in their communication related to work.

Observe how people say it.
In addition to the words, the coach also should pay very close attention to how things are communicated. The tone of voice and body language of the person will usually communicate more than the words themselves.

Observe what people do.
The coach must observe people doing their assigned responsibilities to observe the actual steps they take in the process. Observing what people do may also mean observing what is not being done that should be done.

Observe how people do their job.
When observing how people do their job, the coach should examine the following areas: accuracy, quality, speed, sequence, motivation, how the person is interacting with others to accomplish the task and other related areas.

The Critical Incident

During the observation phase, you are looking for situations or behaviors that you believe relate to the *Performance* or *Behavioral goals* of the person. When you see something specific that you want to discuss, this is called the critical incident. The critical incident is the situation where the specific behavior appears.

The goal of the observation phase is to see the behavior of the individual so that you can know exactly what his behavior is and so that you can help him understand his behavior and how it affects others.

Closing Thoughts

The observation step is critical for your effectiveness as a coach. You must make a habit of blocking time to be with your people just as you block time to be in meetings. This time will be a great investment in helping your people be successful.

Action Step

Establish a plan to observe each person's behavior. Let them know what you will be doing so that there are no surprises. You may want to say something like this:

"Susan, one way that I can help you be successful is to give you accurate feedback on your performance. To do this, I must be able to see you when you are in action. The more I see how you do your job, the better we can dialogue about your performance."

CHAPTER NINE

The Awareness Step
Discussion Performance Issues

To develop self-propelled people, correct behavior must be reinforced and problem behavior must be corrected.

You reviewed performance expectations with Susan in the annual goal setting session. You and Susan left with a clear understanding of the goals to be accomplished and the plan to track her progress. This morning you observed Susan and identified two patterns that you need to discuss with her. One was a very positive thing that she did. The second was a behavior that needs to be adjusted. You have a meeting with her after lunch. You are entering the awareness step of the coaching process.

The awareness phase is the part of the performance coaching process where you dialogue with the individual about what you have observed. Your success as a coach is based largely on your ability to reinforce positive behavior and help your people identify and correct problem behavior.

Performance Coaching Principle #9

Coaching success is based on your ability to rein-force positive behavior and correct problem behavior.

The goals of the awareness step

When you dialogue with people about their performance, there are two goals: awareness and comprehension.

- Awareness –
  Awareness means that you help people see what they have been doing. There are times when people are not really aware of what they are doing. As the leader, you must help them become aware of this. In some cases this will mean describing the be-havior so that there is a clear understanding of what happened. In other cases it may simply mean bringing the behavior to the person's attention.

- Comprehension –
  Once people becomes aware of the behavior, the leader must help them comprehend how the behavior affects others as well as their own success. Many people are aware of their behavior. What they may not understand, though, is how that behavior really affects others, as well as how their behavior is affecting their own success.

You want to leave the awareness phase with the person saying, "I see the behavior and I understand the impact that the behavior has on me, others in the organization and the organization as a whole." In some cases, the awareness and comprehension are positive. In these situations, you want to reinforce the correct behavior. In other situations, awareness and comprehension mean understanding how behavior is negatively impacting success and others in the organization.

When to do the awareness step

The awareness phase can occur whenever you observe a behavior that should be addressed. The awareness phase should be done as soon after the observation phase as possible. The guiding rule is simple: The sooner the better. If you meet quickly after the observation phase, the events are fresh to you and the person. If you observe the person in a meeting, then you should meet with him immediately after the meeting. If you are observing him in a telephone conversation, you should discuss it immediately afterwards if possible. If you are observing him in a private conversation, the awareness phase should be done at the moment you see something you want to explore.

How to reinforce positive behavior

Many times the performance you see is positive and these behaviors should be reinforced through praise. If people know their behavior is correct they will be more inclined to continue such. There is another important reason to reinforce positive behavior: people love praise. One of the most frequently heard comments in feedback sessions is that people do not feel that they are praised enough. This is heard at every level of almost every organization. Apparently, leaders do not understand the tremendous power of positive reinforcement. The 80%, the majority of the people in the workplace, have the capability to be successful. They will not achieve their success potential, however, without consistent coaching and reinforcement. Giving positive reinforcement for correct behavior is a large part of the coaching process.

Positive reinforcement is easy to do and gives you tremendous return on your investment. Three simple guidelines will enhance your use of positive reinforcement and will help your employees improve their performance.

- "The fifteen-second rule"-
  Praising people does not take a lot of time. When done properly, praise should not take any longer than fifteen to sixty seconds. Although some situations may require more time, praise should usually be quick.

- Genuine caring-
  When praising someone's behavior, be very genuine. If you are not genuine and authentic in praise, the person will perceive it as manipulative. In these situations, pseudo-praise can actually have a reverse impact on the person and reduce performance.

- Praise for specific behavior-
  You should recognize specific behavior. Praise how a project was completed. Praise the number of assignments completed. Praise the specific way the person communicated with a customer. Praise how someone organized a project. When you reinforce specific behavior, it communicates to the person exactly what he should do the next time.

  "Susan, you did an excellent job on the Wilson project. Specifically, you did three things that made the project report successful. Your thoughts were very clear, your grammar was excellent and you outlined exactly what needed to be done in the future."

Discussing problem performance

Occasionally, you will need to talk with your people about problem performance. For many leaders this is uncomfortable. Either the leader is uncomfortable addressing problems, or the leader does not know how to start the conversation in a caring way and keep the meeting focused.

To address and resolve these concerns, the leader must have the right mindset and a template to begin the conversation and move it toward the desired goals.

- The right mindset-
  As a leader you must understand that talking with someone about problem performance is a caring act. Many leaders put off discussing problem behavior under the guise that they really care for the person and therefore don't want to create hard feelings or upset them. If you put off addressing problems, it is not because you care for the person, it is because you either don't know how to do it or you are afraid of the confrontation that may occur when you talk about the problem.

  The most caring action you can take for someone is to talk about problem behavior. Discussing problem behavior is a signal that you want the person to be successful. Do not shy away from addressing problems. Your people will thank you because you cared enough to identify areas where they are not being successful.

- A template for conversation-
  Once you have the right mindset, the next step is to plan the introduction and how to keep the conversation moving toward the desired goal of improving performance. There are three simple rules that can assist you in beginning and guiding any conversation:

- Do not assume malicious intent. In most cases, the person is not intentionally trying to fail. Something is keeping him from being successful. It may be internal to the person or it may be something in the work environment. Whatever the case, assume that the intent of the person is good. This will keep you from beginning the conversation in a harsh or accusing way.
- Describe what you saw or what you sense about a situation and ask the person to help you understand what is happening or why he did a certain thing.
- Use the dialogue-planning tree to plan for any potential negative words or actions. If you are prepared for the negative comments of a person, you can better focus on the person and the conversation.

Guiding discussion in the Awareness Step

The following is a template that can guide you through most discussions about problem performance.

- Call what you see-
  "Call what you see" is a technique that allows you to describe a behavior or tell the person what appears to be the real problem from your perspective. Call what you see can serve two useful purposes. First, it can allow you to help   the person clearly define the problem. Second,   it can give the person a graceful out if this is the first or second time that you have talked about this problem. Here is how it is used: *"Susan, I did not get the report that you promised me yesterday afternoon."*

- Help me understand-
  When you discuss performance problems do not jump to conclusions. When you see a problem, describe what you see and ask the person to explain. "Help me understand" is always used in conjunction with "Call what you see." It is literally used just as it sounds: *"Susan, I did not get the report that you promised me yesterday afternoon. Help me understand what happened."*

- VCR – Validate, Clarify, and Refocus -
  When the person begins explaining what happened, you will need to help him explore what he did, the impact that it had on others, and what needs to be done differently in the future.

V – Validate-

In most cases a person will have a logical reason why something was done. If you want to help examine what was done and then what needs to be done, the next time you have to validate intent. If she says, *"I tried but I just had too many things to do,"* then you may need to say, *"Susan, I know that it was a busy day yesterday."* You are validating her feelings or concerns when you say that you understand it was a busy day. You are not excusing her or saying that her actions were right. You are simply saying you understand her concern.

C – Clarify-

Your next step is to better understand what happened and to help her understand the impact of what happened. You want her to be aware of her behavior and understand the impact of her behavior on you, the organization and her success. *"Susan, I know that you had good intentions. Did you understand why I needed the report by yesterday afternoon? What was your understanding? Did you understand how important the report was to me and the organization? What was your understanding? Did I communicate clearly my expectations, because it may be that I was a part of the problem? If you knew that you were not going to get it completed on time, and you knew that it was important, why were you uncomfortable coming to me and letting me know earlier in the day?"* The list of questions you use in the clarification stage may vary depending on the issue and whether this is the first time you have talked about this problem. The intent of this section is to understand if someone is aware of the behavior and to be sure that the person comprehends the impact of his or her actions.

R – Refocus-
The last part of the process is designed to help the person begin thinking about how to correct the problem. The refocus stage leads you naturally into the last stage of performance coaching – The alignment stage. *"Susan, it is important to me that you are successful. Let's look at what we can do the next time to make sure that this problem does not happen again."*

Problems that can occur during the alignment step

If you use the above template, you will find that eighty to ninety percent of your coaching sessions are very positive and constructive. Occasionally, however, your discussion will not go as you planned. It is best to anticipate these and to plan for them using the dialogue-planning tree. As we conclude this chapter, I want to identify the six most common problems that may occur during the alignment step and give you some thoughts on how to address them.

- Person becomes angry-
  Some people, when confronted with performance problems, will become angry. Anger is usually a defense mechanism to mask the person's fear about the situation. If someone does become angry, your first task is to reduce the anger and then to help the person explore why she became angry. You may try the following process:

"Susan, it is obvious that our discussion has made you angry. Help me understand why it has made you angry." (This is "Call what you see" and "Help me understand.")

Anticipate why she is angry in this situation. It is usually because she is embarrassed, she is afraid that her job is in jeopardy, or she is really upset that you or someone else did not do what they were supposed to do and she is getting the blame. Whatever the reason, you should anticipate each of these when planning for the conversation. If you made a mistake, plan to admit it and take appropriate action. In each of these situations, it is important that you help her focus on the things in this situation that are within her control.

- Person begins to cry-

  It is not unusual for some people to cry when they are confronted with performance issues. As strange as this may sound, tears are usually a form of anger. Many people grew up with an understanding that anger was not an appropriate expression. When they felt anger, they had to find some way to express the anger. Tears can also be a reaction to fear. It is important when someone cries that you help him or her examine the reason for the tears so that you can help the person address the problem behavior. The following process is often helpful:

  "Susan, this is obviously an emotional issue for you. That is OK. Take as long as you need." Provide Susan with some tissues and let her cry. Do not try to stop her from crying. This is usually a wasted effort. Once Susan has stopped crying, help her explore why this situation created tears.

  "Susan, help me understand why this was such an emotional issue for you." Or *"Susan, what was it about our conversation that caused you to become upset?"* At this point, you need to understand the root cause of her tears. If it is something within your control, you can make appropriate adjustments. If it

is something that is in her realm of responsibility, you can help her begin to deal with it.

- Person becomes quiet-
Some people become quiet when they are confronted with problem behavior. Like the two previous examples, your task is to examine why they have become quiet. Usually people are quiet because they are afraid or they sense a lack of control over the outcome of a situation.

"Susan, you have been very quiet during our conversation. Help me understand why." When you ask this question, be prepared to wait for the person to talk. Resist the temptation to fill the silence with your words. If you are willing to resist the silence, you will be rewarded with valuable information to help Susan succeed.

- Person disagrees with your assessment-
There will be times when the person will disagree with your assessment of his or her performance. In these settings, you need accurate information and must have observed the person enough to be able to see a pattern of behavior. The best way to eliminate disagreement about performance is to define performance by using *Performance goals* and *Behavioral goals.* If there are still situations where the person disagrees with your assessment of his or her performance, the following conversation may help you:

"Susan, help me understand what part of my assessment or observation you disagree with." Listen carefully to what Susan says. Susan may have isolated one comment that you made and based her entire disagreement on this one comment. If you can understand this, you can help clarify the problem behavior. In these situations it may be useful to say something like the following: *"Susan, it appears that you really disagree with*

*this one statement. Am I right? Let's address this one state-
ment and then I want us to focus on the bigger issues of...”*

Also, listen to determine if Susan's definition of success is the
same as yours. Even when you define *Performance goals* and
Behavioral goals, some people still have their own definition of
success that may not be consistent with yours. *“Susan, when
we talked about... what did we identify as the expected behavior? In our conversation, it appears that you have a
different description of what this behavior should be. Am I
right? Let's clearly define this behavior so that both of us
can agree on exactly what is expected in the future.”*

- Person does not want to admit that he has made a mistake-
  You will find some people who do not want to admit that they
  have made a mistake or that they have exhibited the wrong behavior. This may occur because the person does not want to
  admit an error or there may be a deep seated sense of failure
  associated with admitting a mistake. Help the person understand that making a mistake is not the same as failure. The only
  way to improve is to learn from the mistakes. You may try the
  following approach: *“Susan, do you remember last week
  when we talked about this....?” “I am not saying that everything you are doing is wrong. There is one area, however, that needs to be addressed.” “Susan, don't worry about
  failing or making mistakes. Everyone makes mistakes. The
  thing that you should focus on is learning from your mistakes in order to get better.” “Susan, why is it difficult for
  you to admit that you made a mistake?”*

- Person wants to blame others-
  Blaming others is perhaps the most common problem that occurs in the awareness step. Many people, when confronted
  with problem performance, want to find someone to blame rather
  than identify what they could have done to control their own

success. If someone is blaming others follow these two steps: First, help the person identify the action within his or her control that can be done differently in the future. Second, if other people were a part of the problem, you must help the person develop a strategy to discuss the problem with these persons. Try the following approach: *"Susan, whenever there is a problem, the first step is to examine what was within your control that could have been done differently. Let's look for a moment at what you could have done differently to achieve a different outcome."* Force Susan to examine the things that are within her control. If she cannot identify anything that is within her control, be prepared with a list of the things that are within her control. It may be useful to ask about each one in the following way, *"Susan, is this... within your control?"*

If there are things outside of Susan's control, you should help her develop a strategy to address these areas with the right persons. In most cases, you want to avoid fixing the problem for Susan. Remember, you want Susan to be a self-propelled person. If you fix the problem for her, she will come back to you to fix it in the future.

Closing Thoughts

Addressing problem behavior does not have to be complicated or uncomfortable. If you genuinely care about people and their success, and if you use the simple template above you will quickly address problem performances and your people will usually respond appropriately.

CHAPTER TEN

The Alignment Step
Correcting Performance Problems

People make real changes only when there is an internal conviction that change is essential for their success.

You meet with Susan after lunch to discuss her successful performance and the areas where improvements need to be made. She is motivated by the praise you give her for doing things right. She also recognizes the need for change where there are problems. It is time to transition to the alignment step.

Performance Coaching Principle #10

People change behavior only when their beliefs change.

If you have completed the awareness step successfully, your conversation will naturally move into the alignment step. The alignment step is usually done immediately after the awareness step and is simply seen as a continuation of the conversation by the other person.

The alignment step is the step in which the coach leads the person to recognize that change and helps develop a plan to change such behavior. The alignment step is so named because the purpose of the phase is to help the person align the beliefs and the behavior with the goal behavior needed by the organization. If the awareness step is done properly, the alignment step will be relatively straight-forward and positive.

The goals in the alignment step

The four goals in the alignment step are as follows:
- The person must become personally convinced that change is necessary and make a commitment to change.
- The coach and the individual must develop a strategic plan to improve performance until it reaches the acceptable level.
- The coach and the individual must develop a timeline to implement changes.
- The coach and the person must establish follow-up plans to track and evaluate progress.

The change factors

Helping people change is one of your primary responsibilities as a leader. It is also one of your most rewarding actions. When you see people grow and change in a positive way it empowers not only the people but also others around them. If someone is going to change a behavior, the person must transition through the following four stages:

- Catalyst

  For change to occur, something must cause the person to stop and look at present behavior. We call this the catalyst. A catalyst may be something external to the person or something internal. The inability to get work completed in a timely manner may be an external catalyst. A conversation with a leader or co-worker may be an internal or an external catalyst. A change in the economy can be an external catalyst. A feeling of dissatisfaction with one's career or with relationships may be an internal catalyst. Whether the catalyst is external or internal, it is the event or thought that forces someone to look at what he or she is doing now.

- Awareness

  The next step in the change process is for the person to become aware of the behavior that needs to be changed. Many people do things but do not realize that the behavior is inconsistent with their long-range goals. If the people are going to change, they must become aware of the unacceptable or inappropriate behavior.

- Comprehension

  Change is eighty-percent mental and twenty-percent action. Most people do not change because they do not really believe their behavior needs to be changed or they do not believe they can do anything about it. Once the person makes the mental shift, the change in behavior comes almost automatically. Comprehension is a key step in the process of change. Comprehension means that the person intellectually and emotionally understands the impact of the behavior on others, the organization and his or her own success.

- Conviction

  The final step in the change process is for the person to develop an internal conviction that change is needed. Conviction is a strong belief that the existing behavior must change and a willingness to take specific steps to change that behavior. Without this conviction, the person will not sustain changed behavior. This is the root issue when someone changes behavior for a few weeks or months and then returns to old habits. The person was not really convicted of the need for change. He or she may have changed behavior to please someone but did not really see the need for change on a permanent basis. When someone has a conviction that change is needed and when he or she develops and follows a plan to achieve the change, the behavior will be transformed.

Leading the alignment step

There are seven parts to the alignment step. Each of these steps is described below.

Step: Communicate the need for change.
Comment: The person must understand that change is essential for future success. *"Susan, there will be many days in the future when you will be busy. If you are going to be successful, you must learn how to get the most important work done every day."*

Step: Get agreement on the need for change.
Comment: Be sure that the person understands and agrees to the need for change. *"Susan, do you understand the importance of making changes in this area? Tell me why you think a change is needed. Are you willing to work with me to develop a plan to change your behavior?"*

Step: Define the desired behavior.
Comment: *"Let's define exactly what we are looking for."*

Step: Verify understanding of the desired behavior.
Comment: Get the person to communicate the desired behavior back to you so that you are sure that it is in fact what you desire. *"Susan, just so we are both on the same wavelength, tell me what you understand the desired behavior to be."*

Step: Ask for commitment.
Comment: *"Susan, can I get your commitment to achieve this behavior?"*

Step: Develop an action plan to achieve the desired behavior.
Comment: Make sure that you involve the person or group in the development of the action plan. This must be a plan that they can support.

Step: Develop a follow-up plan.
Comment: A follow-up plan is essential for developing self-propelled people. Remember, the average person must have the correct behavior reinforced consistently over time for it to become a habit.

The importance of a follow-up plan

Once the action plan is complete, you must develop a follow-up plan to help the person track success. The key to a successful follow-up plan is accurately observing behavior and developing the correct frequency of follow-up for the situation. A general rule to assist in planning follow-up can be found in the phrase "frequent to less frequent." In the early stages of follow-up, it should be frequent. In some cases, follow-up should be done every day for at least a few weeks. In other cases the follow-up may be once a week. When you see improvement, decrease the frequency of follow-up. If you are following up every day, back off to every third day. If progress continues, begin doing follow-up once a week and then once a month. If the person knows that you are going to check with him in the future, he will be more likely to continue correct performance. If you continue to follow-up even at less frequent intervals, he still knows that you will eventually follow-up. If you do this enough, correct performance will become habit.

How to get commitment

Commitment to change behavior is a central focus of the alignment step. Without commitment the person will probably not change behavior. The biggest mistake leaders make when getting commitment is not getting the person to commit to specific actions or changes in the future. Instead of committing to change the behavior Susan will usually say, *"I will try harder,"* and the leader accepts that response as appropriate. Never, and I repeat NEVER, simply take someone's comment, "I will try harder," as a commitment to make change. "Trying harder" does not tell you anything about what the person is going to do differently to change behavior. It usually just means that they will be more aware in the future. To get a change in behavior you must ask a follow-up question, *"Susan, I know that you are going to try harder. Let's talk about specifically what you are going to do next time so that this problem does not occur again."* This follow-up question forces Susan to identify specific actions that she will take in the future. If she identifies specific actions, you then have something that you can track and review with her.

In some cases, commitment may not be easy to obtain. In these situations, one of the following techniques may be useful:

- Ask for a series of small commitments-
  One of the basic principles about getting commitment is that some people will make small commitments easier than they will make large commitments. This being the case, get people to commit

to small things along the way. The following questions are designed to get commitment at each step of the journey:

Is the vision something worth aiming toward?

If we can accomplish this vision, would it help us be more productive? We can work out the details as we go. What I need to know now is this: Do you in principle agree with this vision?

- Would you be willing?-
  If you address a problem with someone and you and the person have difficulty coming to an agreement of what needs to be done, "would you be willing" may be a useful tool. This technique allows you to get an agreement from the person to test or try a certain action for a defined period of time. At the end of the time period, you will sit down together and review the results. It sounds like this:

"Susan, since we are having difficulty agreeing on a solution, let me ask you if you would be willing to try ... for the next two weeks to see if it will help? If you are, then let's clarify exactly what you are going to do for the next two weeks and how we will follow-up after the time period is over."

Using consensus decision-making to get commitment or to develop action plans

Sometimes the organization may define the behavior for the person without any real input from the person. The person in these situations simply must commit to do the defined behavior. In other situations it will be important that you and the person define the expected behavior together. In these settings it may be useful to use a consensus decision-making model to define the change needed.

There are many misconceptions about consensus decision making. Consensus decision making means that you and the person agree to work together to establish a goal or make a decision that both of you can support. The following steps can make consensus decision making a positive and productive time for you and your people:

Step: Agree to stay with the process until a decision can be reached that is agreeable to all.
Comment: This does not mean that the decision will be everyone's ideal decision. It is rather a decision that everyone can support and that everyone believes is in the best interest of the organization. *"Susan, it is important that we develop a plan that can help you succeed. Will you commit to stay with this process until we can develop a plan that you can achieve?"*

Step: Define the decision to be made.
Comment: The decision must be stated clearly. *"Susan, we must develop a strategy for you to manage your work so that you can complete essential documents on time."*

Step: Establish criteria for the decision.
Comment: For the decision to be the best decision, it must meet certain criteria. In many cases the criteria may be established for the individual or group by the organization or the leader. In other cases, the person or group will have to establish the criteria. If criteria are not established for the group, then the criteria will fall into two categories:
Essential and Desirable.
Essential criteria are the criteria that everyone agrees must be in the plan. If a plan does not meet all of these criteria, then it is rejected.
Desirable criteria are the criteria that the person or group would like to have in the plan if they have the option.
It will be useful to list each of these criteria and develop a matrix.

Step: Brainstorm decision options.
Comment: During this part of the process, the participants examine all of the possible decisions or plans.

Step: Evaluate each option based on the criteria developed in the previous step.
Comment: If one of the options does not contain all of the essential criteria, then it is not considered.

Step: Agree on a decision.
Comment: Once the options are evaluated, the person or group and the leader must agree on the decision.

The consensus model has a number of benefits. First, it gets the person involved in correcting the problem. It also forces the person to think about his behavior and how to correct it. If the person is involved in the decision, he is more likely to follow the plan.

Alignment step techniques

There are a few techniques that you may find useful in the alignment step, particularly if you are addressing the same problem more than once.

- Either/Or
  This technique is particularly helpful when you have addressed a problem with someone numerous times. The "either/or" technique helps to narrow down potential problems or causes so you can understand the real issue. It also lets you put the responsibility for the problem in the right place: on the person's shoulders. The "either/or" technique goes like this:

  "Susan, help me understand. Either I did not explain the task properly or you were preoccupied and were not listening? Which one is it?"

"Susan, this is the third time we have talked about this problem. Either you don't think we are serious or you just don't want to do it. Which one is it?"

- Define reality-
  The goal of any coaching session is to help people take responsibility for their actions and take the initiative to do what they are supposed to do in their job. Many times, this is difficult. Some people do not want to perform the tasks they were hired to do. If you find yourself with this type of person, defining reality may be a useful technique to help him grow. The technique goes something like this:

  "It appears to me that you do not think that this ... is a part of your job. Is that true? It is important for you to understand that this ... is a part of your job, and if you cannot do this, then we need to talk about whether you are right for this job."

- Do you want this job?
  You may never have to use this technique, but occasionally you will have someone that just resists making changes. If you have done everything you know to do and still there is no results, you may have to use this technique. The technique goes like this:

  "Susan, we have talked about this problem six times now and I see no improvement. This is an essential part of your job. If you do not or cannot do this, this job is not right for you. Let me ask you this question, 'Do you want this job?' If you want this job you have to do this task."

Closing Thoughts

Remember, most people want to be successful. Most people also need some guidance and direction if they are going to achieve success. One of your jobs as a leader is to help them address problem behavior and correct that behavior until the desired success is achieved.

CHAPTER ELEVEN

Eliminating Reoccurring Problems

Reoccurring problems are more of a leadership issue than a person issue.

One of the frustrating situations many leaders face is reoccurring problems. These are the problems that just don't seem to go away. These are the persons who continue to perform at a less than desirable level. These are the persons who may improve for a period of time and then return to less than adequate performance. Reoccurring problems are the most frustrating part of coaching people because you want the person to be successful. If you have these frustrations, there is good news! There is a way to eliminate reoccurring problems if you are willing to do some very specific things.

The secret to resolving reoccurring problems

Performance Coaching Principle #11

Reoccurring problems are a leadership issue more than a people issue.

You must first realize that reoccurring problems are a leadership problem more than an employee problem. Before you get too upset let me explain by looking at how problems reoccur.

Each person comes into the job with certain expectations of the job and related duties. Each person also brings an individual personality and habits to the job. At the same time the organization also has certain expectations of the job. Included in expectations is a defined set of skills and knowledge, which the person should possess and use. Quite often the expectations of the person and the organization differ.

In an effective organization, these expectations are clearly defined. A follow-up plan is developed to track these expectations. Training is provided if needed, and the leader coaches the person to reinforce the right behavior and correct problem behavior. If the problem behavior continues after training and coaching, the leader discusses the problem in more depth. The leader must determine if the person is really capable of doing the job in the prescribed manner. If any step in this process is missing, the potential for creating reoccurring problems is present.

In all of these cases, the person who is responsible for defining expectations, holding the person accountable to the expectations and coaching the person is the leader. In most cases the real problem in reoccurring problems is one of the following issues:

- Expectations have never clearly been defined.
- The problem has not been addressed in the past.
- The person really does not have the skills needed to do the job.
- The person has not been adequately trained to do the job.
- The leader has not developed a follow-up plan so problems can quickly be addressed.
- The leader has addressed the problem but never attached serious consequences if the behavior continues. This last one is like the child who gets his hand caught in the cookie jar. His mother spanks him and says, "Don't do that again." Nothing else happens, however, except another spanking when he is caught again. The child eventually learns that the parent is really not going to do anything different, so the behavior must really not be that bad. The spanking is worth enduring in order to get the cookie.

Follow-up is the key

Follow-up is the best way to correct reoccurring problems. If people know that you will be discussing the problem behavior with them again at a set time, they will usually improve the performance at least until the next meeting. One of the ways that you can help someone improve their performance is to continue follow-up. The strategy should always be frequent to less frequent. For example: If you talk with someone about a problem today, plan to meet tomorrow afternoon or in a few days to discuss it again. If the person is improving, schedule another follow-up in a few days. Do this a few times. If the person continues to exhibit the desired behavior, lengthen the meetings to once a week. If things are going well, move follow-up to once a month. Finally, address the issue in your quarterly performance coaching.

The "two tell rule" is a helpful tool

One frustration associated with reoccurring problems is that the leader talks about the same problem over and over. There is a simple way to eliminate talking about the same problem over and over. We call it the "two tell rule." The "two tell rule" eliminates having the same conversation over and over again. The "two tell rule" says that you should only tell someone what needs to be done twice. After telling twice, you should switch to a questioning approach. The "two tell rule" is a very simple rule based on the principle of accountability. When most leaders discuss problems they talk, talk, talk. The leader tells the person to improve and the person says he will try harder. The problem with this approach is that accountability is not really placed on the shoulders of the person. If you want self-propelled people, you must help the person be accountable for his own actions. To do this, he must talk about what he is going to do different. To get him to talk, you must ask questions.

Unless someone is a new employee, there is no need for you to tell someone about a problem behavior more than twice. Once you have told someone twice you should shift to a questioning mode. Continue in that questioning mode until the behavior changes or he admits that he is not going to do the desired behavior. The "two tell rule" is used in the following way:

"Susan, twice we have sat down and talked about this issue. What did we discuss in both of those sessions? What did you say you would do? Why is it still not being done?"

The value of the "two tell rule" is simple. If the person knows what needs to be done, it shifts the responsibility for actions to his shoulders.

Be Specific

Another useful tool is being specific. When you confront someone about performance problems, the tendency is for the person to say that he will "try harder." While the intentions of the person are probably good when he makes this comment, it tells you nothing about what he is going to do different in the future to achieve greater results. To help the person become committed to taking a specific action, you will have to be more specific with the person.

If Susan does say that she will try harder, respond in the following way:

"Susan, I know that you are going to try harder. But I need to ask you, 'What specifically are you going to do differently in the future to keep this from happening again.'" Forcing the person to be specific will enable her to develop a specific plan that can be used in the future. It also will provide you with a "hook" to which you can return if the defined action is not performed. Should Susan not do what she said she would do, you have a natural avenue to discuss the problem. *"Susan, last week when we talked about this problem, you said that you were going to do this... Tell me what has happened."*

The three step process for eliminating reoccurring problems

There are three steps to eliminating reoccurring problems. These steps are based on the assumption that expectations have been clearly defined with the person in the past. If *Performance goals* and *Behavioral goals* have not been established in the past, you must go back and do this first.

Step One

- You observe problem behavior.
- Call what you see – *"Susan, I was reading your report yesterday and you did not include the section on productivity that we agreed should be in the report."*
- Help me understand – *"Help me understand why it is not in the report."*
- VCR – *"Susan, I understand that it was a busy day for you."* (You are validating her busy day.) *"Do you understand how important that information is to the rest of the organization? Everything we plan for the next week is driven by that information. What is keeping you from getting this information entered on time?"* (You are clarifying so that she understands the importance of the material and she examines why she is not able to get it to you on time.) *"Even though your week is busy, this information must be completed and emailed to me by Friday. Let's talk about how you are going to do that. Are there skills that you need to learn? Is there knowledge that I need to share with you?"*
- Set a follow-up meeting – *"Susan, let's meet next Thursday and see how things go next week."*

Step Two

- Performance problem occurs again.
- Call what you see – with a reminder that we discussed this problem last week. *"Susan, last week we talked about this same problem. Here we are again on Thursday and the information is not going to be ready for tomorrow."*
- Help me understand – *"Susan, help me understand what happened. I thought we had a clear understanding of what needed to be done."*
- VCR – *"Susan, I understand that this is a lot of work* (validate her concern), *but as we discussed last week, we have to figure out how to get it done and still do the other things you need to do. Let's look at what happened this week* (clarify).

Susan, what are you going to do differently so that I have this information on time next week?" (refocus)

Step Three

- Performance problem occurs for the third time.
- Use the questioning approach – "Susan, *twice before we have talked about this subject. On both occasions what did we talk about? What did you say you would do?"*
- I am confused and Either/Or – *"Susan, I am confused. Both times when we talked, I understood that you knew what needed to be done and that you were going to do certain things. Either I misunderstood or you were not serious about your commitment to do certain things. Which one is it?"*
- Define Reality – *"Susan, if you are going to be successful in this job, you must learn how to get this information to me when I need it. If you cannot get the material to me on time, you either are not capable of doing so or you really don't want to do it. Which one is it?"*
- Understand consequences – *"Do you understand the conse- quences of not getting this material to me on time? What are the consequences?"* It is important for the person to un- derstand that if the problem occurs again that there will be spe- cific consequences that will follow.
- Do you want this job? – *"Susan, you need to decide whether or not you really want this job. If you do, this is what is required in the job ..."*
- Your success is your responsibility – *"Susan, I want you to be successful, but I cannot make you successful. Ultimately, your success is your responsibility."*

The third step in this process may actually occur over a few meet- ings. The point of the third step is this: If the person is competent, then you do not need to "tell him" what to do more than twice. Every meeting thereafter, whether it is one meeting or five, should be driven by questions, instead of telling again.

Let me give a word of caution about having too many step three meetings: If you talk in "step three tone" many times and nothing really happens to the person, he will come to believe that his behavior is disliked but not really serious.

Section II
Performance Coaching Principles

Performance Coaching Principle #6
Regular feedback is the key to long-term success.

Performance Coaching Principle #7
Success requires clearly defined goals and expectations.

Performance Coaching Principle #8
To give accurate feedback on performance you must observe your people.

Performance Coaching Principle #9
Coaching success is based on your ability to reinforce positive behavior and correct problem behavior.

Performance Coaching Principle #10
People change behavior only when their beliefs change.

Performance Coaching Principle #11
Reoccurring problems are a leadership issue more than a people issue.

Section III

Skill Clinics

Essential Skills for Building
Self-propelled People

Understanding the coaching role and mindset is not enough. You must also acquire the right skills. Skills are simply resources and tools which aid in your success. The right beliefs without the right skills are like a ship with a great breeze and a great captain, but no sails to catch the wind.

Helping people become self-propelled means that you have to do something different. To do something different, you must learn a new set of skills. Section three covers the essential skills you need to be an effective coach.

CHAPTER TWELVE

Thinking Strategically

*What organizations say they want and what they encourage
are often two different things.*

The importance of thinking strategically

Performance Coaching Principle #12

To develop self-propelled people, you must learn to think strategically.

Do you remember Performance Coaching Principle #5? It says that belief always precedes behavior. People act the way they do because of how they think. For example, if people take responsibility for their own actions they do so because they believe this is the right action. This same principle, belief precedes behavior, applies to leaders as well as those who work with them. How you as a leader thinks is the most important dimension of your success, especially if your goal is to develop self-propelled people. What you think about your role and responsibilities as a leader will, to a large degree, determine your success.

One part of "right thinking" is learning to think strategically. Thinking strategically means that you focus on the mission, vision and goals of your organization and how your actions affect these goals.

Why strategic thinking is essential

For many years, strategic thinking was thought to be the responsibility of only "upper management." Everyone else was supposed to simply implement upper management's plan. This view is very, very outdated. The decentralized workplace of today demands that leaders throughout the organization learn to think strategically.

Strategic thinking is also essential if you want to develop self-propelled people. Your people must believe that you know where you are going and how you plan to get there. They cannot focus on the goals and the plans if they do not know what they are. If your people do not believe that you support the goal, they will become hesitant. When they become hesitant, they will not act on their own initiative. If you understand the goals but have no plan to accomplish them, they will likewise become hesitant. Obviously, hesitant people are not self-propelled people.

Unfortunately, many leaders, because of cultural conditioning, have developed "task thinking." Task thinking focuses only on the next task to be done without considering the impact of this task on others. This style of thinking causes people to put on mental blinders. Leaders who think in such a manner will become passive and wait for direction instead of becoming proactive. A proactive leader can assess what needs to be done in a situation and take appropriate action. "Task thinking" can also cause leaders to believe that the end (the goal or task) justifies the means (I can use whatever method it takes to get the job done).

The key to thinking strategically

The real key to thinking strategically is changing your fundamental belief about what the organization wants from you as a leader. Your job is to use your head! Your job is to think! Your responsibility is to be proactive and not just wait passively for someone to give you direction. Passive leaders cannot develop self-propelled people.

If you want to be a strategic thinker you must be able to do the following:

- Understand the goals of your organization.
- Be committed to these goals.
- Understand how your group relates to these goals.
- Develop goals and plans with your people that are consistent with the organization's goals.
- Understand the impact of your actions on your organization and the organization's goals and objectives.
- Think in terms of "how you can" rather than "why you can't."
- Develop action steps to be sure that your goals are coordinated with the goals of other parts of the organization.

The magic eight

Answering eight essential questions can help you learn to think strategically. We call this set of questions the "magic eight." There is really nothing magical about the questions, but powerful and positive things happen when you and your people answer these questions before the start of every project.

- *What are we doing?* (Task)
  You and your people must have a clear understanding of the goal that you are to accomplish and the specific tasks required.

- *Why are we doing it?* (Reason)
  Self-propelled people need to know why a certain action is needed.
- *How are we doing it?* (Method)
  If there is a specific way the task needs to be done, this should be communicated to everyone. However, if the method is open for discussion then the leader and the people performing the task should agree on how the task should be done.
- *When are we doing it?* (Timeline)
  Is there a specific timeline for completing the task? This information is essential at the beginning of each project. Knowing the timeline will help your people manage their time and task more efficiently.
- *Who needs to be involved?* (Participants)
  Before any project begins, everyone who relates to the project should be involved in the planning of the project. This means that suppliers, customers and the people doing the work should all have input into the process. Better input and planning creates better products and services.
- *What is everyone's role?* (Roles)
  Defining everyone's role before the project begins can simplify matters from the beginning and make everyone's job more productive and enjoyable.
- *How will this affect others?* (Impact)
  Strategic thinking is not complete without assessing the impact of your actions on others. This means that each person must understand the impact of his or her actions on others in the group. The group must also consider the impact of its actions on other groups within the organization.
- *What if this… happens?* (Contingencies)
  The last question is designed to help you and your people anticipate problems that can occur and how to address them.

How to think strategically

The following steps can help you develop strategic thinking:

- *Develop a clear understanding of and commitment to the mission and vision of the organization.*
  Strategic thinking requires that you buy into the mission and vision of the organization. This means more than token commitment. If you are not clear about the mission and vision of your organization, meet with the people in your organization who can clarify these for you. If you have questions or concerns related to the mission and vision of your organization, address these now with the right people. Make sure your people also understand and support the mission and vision of your organization.

- *Develop a clear understanding of and commitment to the goals and strategic plans of the organization.*
  Strategic plans and goals represent "how" the mission and vision are to be accomplished. As a coach you must emotionally buy into the goals of the organization. You must also understand, support and communicate these plans and goals to your people if they are to become self-propelled.

- *Develop a clear understanding of how your subgroup relates to the mission, vision and goals of the organization.*
  Once you have a clear understanding of the organizational goals, you must understand how your group relates to the mission and goals of the organization. Your people must understand how their roles relate to the big picture and how each part of the organization relates to each other. This is called the "chain of connection." You must understand this connection, and be able to communicate this connection to your people in such a way that they understand and act appropriately themselves. This step will usually involve dialogue with people inside and outside your department.

- *Develop goals in your subgroup that are consistent with the organization's mission, vision and goals.*
  It is essential that your group's goals be consistent with your organization's larger goals. It is also essential that your people be involved in the development and implementation of these goals. Many leaders have a tendency to wait on their managers to give them goals. Don't wait! Begin thinking yourself about what your department or group is capable of achieving in relation to the vision and goals of the organization. This proactive approach will help you begin to develop the same proactive mindset in your people.

- *Communicate the goals with everyone in your subgroup and within your organization.*
  Communication is a central element in developing self-propelled people. If your people are informed, they can take appropriate action because they know the target. Talk often about the goals with your people. Update people regularly on progress toward these goals. It is also useful to communicate these goals to others in the organization whose actions affect you. If others know your goals, they can possibly assist you in achieving them.

- *Develop strategies or plans to achieve these goals.*
  Goals are useless without strategies to achieve them. These strategies are simply the methods the group will use to achieve goals. Leaders often ask, "Should I involve my people in the development of strategies?" There is a simple rule of thumb in this matter. If the strategy is going to affect your people, they will buy into it more if they have some input into the strategy.

- *Develop follow-up plans to reinforce the strategy.*
  Accountability is an essential part of building self-propelled people. People will do what is reinforced. If you regularly follow-up to evaluate performance in a specific area, people will begin to act in the desired manner. Growing a healthy loan port-

folio is a good example. If you only focus on growing the port-folio size, people may secure marginal or questionable loans. If you focus on both loan quality and loan volume you will create a healthy portfolio.

Aids to reinforce strategic thinking

Here are some other thoughts that may help you reinforce strategic thinking.

- Talk frequently about the goals and the strategies to achieve the goals.
- Get your people to evaluate the effectiveness of the strategies on a regular basis. In other words, "Is it working like we want it to work?" This will help your people become strategic thinkers.
- Be willing to make adjustments yourself if it will help reinforce the strategy. This will send a signal that you are committed.
- Get your people together to talk about the strategy themselves. This means that it is not necessary for you to be present all of the time in these meetings.
- Be upbeat and positive about the goals and strategies.
- When the strategy is successful, recognize this success and reward the people in some way.
- Get feedback from customers. Make sure that some of your people are involved in this communication.

Closing Thoughts

Stay focused on the right goals. Many leaders lose sight of the real goal and get caught up in being right and telling people what to do. Don't worry about being right. Be concerned about helping your people achieve their goals. If you have to adjust – adjust. If you need to flex – flex. Remember, the goal is to develop self-propelled people. Many leaders have sacrificed self-propelled people because they were more interested in proving that they were right.

Action Step

Identify the areas where you need to begin thinking strategically. Follow the steps in this chapter to begin now thinking strategically about your organization and your role in it.

CHAPTER THIRTEEN

Building an Intentional Work Culture

"If you build it, he will come." From *Field of Dreams*

I recently worked with an organization that was experiencing significant change. They were involved in a growth cycle, which meant upgrading their technology and processes. We were leading a series of listening sessions throughout the organization to assess how they were managing the change and to identify ways they could manage change more effectively in the future.

The first step of the process was to meet with leaders to define the type of work culture and the type of people that they really wanted in the organization. Throughout many listening sessions we evaluated the comments of their people to see if the structure and culture of the organization were achieving the results they desired and helping them develop the type of persons they needed. The answer was clearly "no." The leaders wanted an organization where everyone was cooperating to achieve a common goal and where people were exhibiting self-starter characteristics. Like all leaders, they wanted self-propelled people. However, the organization was structured to do something completely different. There were no set communication meetings to keep people informed. Training was ineffective and not reinforced consistently. No regular systems were in place to give people feedback on their performance more than once a year. The people did not understand the "chain of connection" within the organization and how everyone related to others. Leaders were encouraging people to "do what they were told, don't rock the boat and don't ask questions." While the intention of the leaders was good, their actions were leading people away from what they said they wanted.

The Alignment Principle

The situation described above is fairly common in many organizations. People say they want one thing, but their daily actions reinforce something else. With the best of intentions, organizations do the opposite of what they say they want. If you want self-propelled people, it is essential that your organization be designed to encourage self-propelled people. This is called the principle of alignment.

Performance Coaching Principle #13

The Alignment Principle - For you to achieve maximum success, how you do things must be consistent with your beliefs and goals.

In simple terms, the principle of alignment means that one of your responsibilities as a leader is to examine your work culture and your leadership patterns to see what they reinforce and encourage. If they encourage something besides what you desire, you must be prepared to make adjustments so that your culture and your leadership patterns reinforce your goals.

The alignment principle leads to the building of an intentional work culture. Building an intentional work culture means that you develop structures and systems that move you toward your mission and goals. Doing this requires that you think strategically. You must have a clear understanding of your mission and goals. You must be able to honestly assess your existing performance and recognize when parts of it are inconsistent with where you want to go. You must be able to recognize when your existing systems and structures are helping you accomplish your goals and when they are hindering you from accomplishing your goals.

Developing your cultural vision

Your people will do what you reinforce. If you desire self-propelled people, you must develop a culture that reinforces self-propelled behavior. The first step in this process is developing a cultural vision.

The cultural vision is the way in which you want your people to communicate, coordinate, and cooperate to achieve success. It is the organizational equivalent to what you did in Chapter One. In Chapter One you were asked to clearly define the type of people you seek in your organization. Now, you are defining the culture that you desire. Obviously, these two should relate closely.

The following questions or actions can assist in developing this vision:
- Review the mission, vision, values, and goals of your organization to see what they state or imply about the culture desired.
- Identify the beliefs people need if they are going to be successful and if the organization is going to be successful.
- Identify how you want people to work together. It is important that you be specific when answering this question. If any of your

comments are vague or open for different interpretation, rede-
fine them in a more specific way.

- Define how you want people to identify, address and resolve
problems and conflicts.
- Identify how you want people to work with customers, suppliers and internal business partners.
- Identify what is negotiable and what is not negotiable in the culture. Put another way, "what can be changed and what cannot
be changed?"

Commit to the vision at all levels
of the organization.

Once the cultural vision is defined, the next step is to get commitment to the vision at all levels of the organization. In the initial stages,
this commitment must be made with the key leaders in the organization. Next, other leaders in the organization must become committed
to the vision. Finally, everyone in the organization must commit to
make the vision a reality. The following steps can help you get
commitment:

- _Review the vision._
Make sure that everyone understands the organization's vision
and how it will impact the organization. This should be done in
listening sessions where people can discuss the vision.
- _Discuss why the vision is important._
Instead of telling people why the vision is important, it may be
useful to ask your people– "Why do you think this vision is
important?" Listen to your people so that you know they really
understand why this vision is important.
- _Do a benefit analysis._
Examine the benefits of developing this work culture. It is important for people to understand how the vision is going to benefit them specifically. The following questions may be useful in

this discussion:

If we develop this culture, how would it help you in your day to day work?

How would it impact your performance?

How would it impact our organization's performance?

- *Discuss how the vision is similar and different from the present environment.*

  In most organizations, parts of the vision are already in place. There are many ways in which people are already consistent with the new vision. Affirm the positive behavior. People are more likely to change if they understand that some of the things expected in the new culture are already being done now. It is also important that people understand how the new vision will be different from the existing culture. These are the areas in which you will need to coach your people.

- *Discuss how the people feel or what people think about the cultural vision.*

  Before people commit to the vision they should be able to express how they feel or think about it. This may be positive or negative. Listen to both. Many times the negative comments or concerns will tell you things you need to improve or rethink.

- *Address concerns that people have about making change.*

  People will often not make changes unless they have a chance to discuss their concerns. Recognize that you may not be able to resolve all of their concerns. The key is for them to know that you are listening to their concerns and addressing what is within your control.

- *Identify changes needed in you as a leader.*

  If you need to make changes as the leader, identify these and begin making changes so that they can see your commitment.

- *Ask for commitment.*

  At this point, people should have a clear understanding of the culture desired. The final step is to ask for their commitment to turn this vision into reality. If you have done a good job of defining the vision and discussing the vision with your people, getting commitment should be easy. When asking for commitment, make sure that you do the following things:

– Ask each person specifically if they are willing to work to turn the vision into reality.
– If you sense apprehension or ambivalence to achieve the vision, address it immediately.
– Establish a follow-up plan to review commitment to the vision.

Identify when you are consistent and inconsistent with the desired culture

Defining the vision and getting commitment are the easy parts. The most demanding step is to honestly assess your organization and your personal behavior. It will be tempting to avoid this part of the process. You must, however, assess both your existing culture and your personal behavior. If you do not alter behavior that is inconsistent with your desired goal, your people will not become self-propelled. Somehow, we develop the mistaken notion that our people listen primarily to our words. They do not. Your people mostly watch what you do. If your actions and words are consistent, they believe your actions. If, though, your words and actions are inconsistent, they will always believe your actions.

The following process can help you evaluate your existing culture:

• List the specific behaviors and characteristics that you desire in your culture.
• For each behavior ask this question, "Does our existing culture encourage people to ....?" If the answer is yes, then you must explain why your existing culture does encourage the desired behavior. If the answer is no, you must identify the behavior that the existing culture encourages.
• Have all of the leaders in your organization do this same task.

Meet as a group to review their observations.

- If the culture does not encourage the desired behavior or characteristic, you must identify the actions the organization must take to achieve the desired behavior. This process may be painful, but it is essential if you want self-propelled people. An example may help. Last year I worked with a client who was developing a team culture. The organization wanted the teams to make decisions related to their day-to-day work. The system, however, did not encourage people to stop and meet. Some team members had received team training while others had not. Performance was only discussed once a year with each person. These were only a few of the ways that the organization was inconsistent with the culture that it desired.

- The same process must be used to examine your leadership patterns. Do your actions encourage people to be self-propelled or do they encourage compliance? An example may be relevant. I recently worked with a client who was changing to a team culture. The leader said he was committed to the team culture. When I met with his people, though, I discovered that his words were inconsistent with his actions. He was not communicating all relevant information with his people. He was not teaching his people the necessary skills to be successful. He was not following up on team issues that were outside of the team's control. Once he realized this inconsistency and made the necessary adjustments, the team's performance dramatically improved.

Get feedback

The best way to know if you are in alignment with the desired culture and goals is to get feedback from your people. Establish regular meetings with your people to hear their perspectives. Let me give you one word of caution, though. Do not argue with their comments. Your people may see you differently than you see yourself.

Should this occur, remember that your intentions are probably good, but your actions may not come across as you intended. The key to making change is listening carefully to what they say. If they need something different than what you presently provide, ask for specific information about what they desire in your behavior. As long as you listen to your people, accept their comments, and make adjustments, your people will begin to develop the characteristics you desire.

Action Step

Meet with other leaders to discuss the existing culture in your organization. Evaluate your existing culture to determine if it supports the culture you desire.

CHAPTER FOURTEEN

Breakdown Analysis

To help people improve their performance, you must first understand what makes up correct performance.

Frequently, we will interview people to assess how effectively an organization is working. One set of questions that we usually ask relates to the effectiveness of leaders. We often hear the following frustration about leaders: "My leader brought me into his office and told me I had to improve, but he would not tell me what I needed to do differently to improve. He simply said, 'Do better or you are out the door.' I want to be successful, but I am not sure what I need to improve."

This frustration is far too common in most organizations. Leaders want their people to improve, but they do not provide specific data or guidance to help them know where to focus their energy and effort to be successful. If you want to turn your 80% into self-propelled people, it will require that you give them specific information that they can use to focus their energy in the right direction.

Identifying the real source of performance problems

Performance Coaching Principle #14

Breakdown Analysis – To help people improve, you must be able to identify the specific actions or beliefs that need to be changed.

Your objective as a coach is to help your people improve their performance. To do this you must isolate the specific areas that need to be improved. One way to identify specific behaviors is to use the breakdown analysis process.

Breakdown analysis is a process that helps you breakdown or subdivide a behavior into its component parts and then identify the desired behavior in each component part. A sports analogy may be the simplest example.

Professional baseball players will occasionally have a batting slump. Just as the name implies, a batting slump occurs when someone is not batting as well as he normally does for an extended period of time. When a player goes into a batting slump, the batting coach will spend many hours watching the batter to see if he can identify specific things that the batter can do differently to pull himself out of the slump. Many times the change is something that we would describe as a "small change" – how he holds his elbow or how he holds his head. These small changes are often what it takes to improve someone's performance.

The batting coach was actually using a breakdown analysis to identify the different parts that make up a good batting average: the stance, the swing, the batters beliefs and thoughts, good concentration, learning to anticipate the type of pitch that will be thrown, learning how to choose good pitches at which to swing, etc. The batting coach then evaluates each of these different parts to see what the person is doing in each area. Success at improving a batting average is usually a combination of improving a number of areas, yet each area must be isolated if the improvements are to be made.

Mindset and Mechanics

Mindset

Improving performance always involves change in two areas: mindset and mechanics. Mindset refers to how the person thinks. Mindset includes the beliefs the person has about himself, his job, his task, the organization, and other related issues. Mindset also includes the focus or concentration that the person has for the particular task. If someone is experiencing performance problems, the person's mindset is usually part of the problem. This is particularly true when you know that the person has the skills or the capability to do the assigned task.

A relevant example may be of value. I recently worked with the CEO of an organization that was trying to improve its financial status. The leader was one of the brightest and most outgoing leaders I have ever met. She carried herself like a true leader when I was around her. When I talked with her people, though, I discovered that there was one trait that was undermining everything that she did. She would avoid conflict like the plague. Because of this aversion to conflict, this individual would put off making decisions related to problems in the organization. This inability to deal with problems was a major morale issue in the organization. It was costing the organization thousands of dollars every year. One day, when we were in a private coaching session, I asked the individual, "Have you ever had a situation where a conflict created a major career problem for you?" The person very quickly identified a time early in her career (twenty years ago) when a conflict had cost her a job. Rather than learn from the conflict and move on, she had become immobilized by the fear. From that point on, she would procrastinate on addressing conflicts until they became major issues. On the surface everything looked great. Under pressure, though, she could not perform.

This person had the capability to deal with conflict. She even understood the mechanics of dealing with conflict. I know this because she was in one of our conflict management seminars and I saw her perform. Her mindset was her stumbling block. Until she overcame the fear of conflict, she would never master the ability to resolve conflict effectively.

The three most common mindset issues you will encounter in your people are lack of self-confidence, fear and lack of interest or desire. Lack of self-confidence is probably the greatest mindset issue that leaders encounter. While lack of self-confidence is actually a form of fear, it is separated because it is arguably the most dominant mindset issue that you will encounter. Many people do not perform at the desired level because they lack the self-confidence to act appropriately in key situations. If people do not have the personal belief in their ability, they will be hesitant to act. This hesitancy to act usually creates the foundation for failure.

People can mask lack of self-confidence in a number of ways, many of which appear to be confident. Carrying oneself with a sense of bravado is one of the most obvious ways to mask insecurity. People try to portray themselves as the toughest, the coolest, the meanest, etc. Another mask for insecurity is always staying busy. If you have someone who is always busy but never getting the right things done, you have a mindset issue. Someone who is always making excuses is also suffering at the core from a lack of confidence. The class clown, the person who is always making fun even at inappropriate times, is usually dealing with a lack of self-confidence. "If I can keep them laughing, they won't see my fears," is what the person is thinking.

Fear is also a major mindset issue. If people are afraid of failure they will be hesitant to act. Fear of failure usually stems from previous life experiences that were so painful that the person seeks to avoid them rather than learn to conquer them. People who are naturally introverted, for example, will often avoid situations where they have to be in front of large groups or where they have to think on their feet in front of people. Avoiding this experience only tends to make the fear larger and immobilize the person even more.

For some people, fear of success is as significant as fear of failure. All people have a mental image of who they are. If they go beyond that image, they either have to change their mental image or shift their behavior in reverse until their actions are again consistent with their mental image. People who are afraid of success will always create a way to fail when they get too far beyond their mental image of themselves.

Lack of interest or desire is the last significant mindset issue that you will encounter. Lack of interest is fundamentally different than a lack of self-confidence or a fear of failure. If people are not interested in the job, they will not focus their energy on being successful in the job. When this occurs, they will not be as successful as they could be. When our oldest son was a senior in high school, he was taking calculus. At one point he became concerned because he was not achieving the grade that he desired. We talked a great deal about the issue. At the core of the problem was a definite lack of interest. He could not understand how he would ever use the class again in his life. Because of this, he did not have a real interest in the course. It showed.

Here are some simple actions you can take to determine if the mindset of the person is a part of the problem:

- First, assess if the person really has the skills to do the tasks. It may even be helpful at this point to provide re-training for the person to ensure that the skills are present.
- Second, assess if the person has the relevant knowledge to accomplish the task.
- Third, make sure that you are consistently reinforcing the desired behavior in a positive way.

If you are doing these three steps and the problem behavior continues, the mindset of the person is likely the issue.

If you do think that the mindset of the person is the issue, here are some steps to help you address the mindset problem:

- First, do not berate, belittle or demean the person. While this may temporarily change the person's behavior, it will never provide long-term change.
- Second, ask a question that affirms the person's capability and opens the door for understanding. *"Bill, I know that you have the skills to do this right, but something seems to be getting in the way. Can you help me understand what is keeping you from doing this task correctly?"*
- Third, continue to ask questions to understand the real issue. *"Bill, are you afraid that you will fail, or are you just not interested in this type of work?"*
- Fourth, when you believe that you have identified the real issue, ask the person what he or she can do to correct the problem.

Mechanics

Many times the issue is the mechanics or "how" the person is doing his or her job. In some cases, skill training will correct the problem. In other cases, the person may know the skill but there is a problem with how the skills are applied. This is where the breakdown analysis can be very useful. The breakdown analysis identifies the problem behavior, compares it with the desired behavior and identifies where the problem lies. There are four steps in the breakdown analysis:

- Identify the performance or behavioral problem.
  In this first step identify the problem that needs to be corrected. *Bill is not achieving the six sales that he must achieve each month. Susan's accuracy is twenty percent below expectation. The morale in Joe's department is deteriorating.*
- Define the desired performance or behavior.
  To identify where the problem lies you must be able to compare the problem behavior or goal to the desired goal. *Bill must achieve six sales a month. Susan should achieve a 98% accuracy. Joe's people should be excited about their daily tasks.*
- Breakdown or subdivide the desired behavior into its component parts.
  This is the critical step. You must identify the steps that are needed to achieve the desired performance or behavior. For example: if the goal is a sales goal, you must define the steps in the sales process and define how each step should be carried out. If the goal is a customer service goal you must define clearly what the process should look like. If you are addressing a leadership issue, you must identify the different steps the leader should take to set the right tone or mood in the department. Each step should then be described in detail so that you know how each step should be done.
- Examine the existing performance of the person to identify where the problem exists.
  If you have done a good job of breaking down each step of the process, you should be able to isolate where the person is having a problem. Without the third step, this last step is more guesswork than solid analysis.

With the information gleaned in the breakdown analysis, you and the person can easily develop a strategy to improve performance. It is useful in most settings to work on one skill area at a time. If you try to improve more than one area at a time, you are not exactly sure what produced the improvement.

Action Step

Identify a performance issue you should address with someone. Do a breakdown analysis to clearly identify where the problem is and how it needs to be corrected.

CHAPTER FIFTEEN

Listening

Hearing people is the easy part. Understanding them is another matter indeed!

Most all of us, at some point, have one of those humbling experiences when you realize that you are not as effective at something as you think you are. Mine was all about listening. In the early days of our marriage, I was on the go constantly. This included when Patty, my wife, was talking to me. Patty would start talking about something and midway through the conversation I would begin to turn away and do something else while she was talking. It always irritated her. "John, are you listening to me?" she would ask. "Of course I am, dear," I would say.

This went on for a number of years. Finally, her frustration got the best of her. We were in the middle of a conversation. She was telling me something she wanted me to do. I began to walk away as she was continuing to give me directions. As I reached the other side of the room, I realized that she was not talking anymore and I turned around. She was standing with her hands on her hips looking straight at me. "Tell me what I just said," she said.

I was caught. I not only could not tell her what she had just said, but I realized that I had developed a pattern of not really listening to her at all. Imagine that. Someone who teaches others how to listen and communicate effectively was not even practicing these things in his own marriage!

Definition of listening

Performance Coaching Principle #15

Listening - caring enough about an individual or group to really understand them and their needs.

Listening is one of the most important communication skills for developing self-propelled people. Paradoxically, listening is also one of the most difficult communication skills to learn because listening requires that you focus your energy and attention outside yourself. It requires a level of self-confidence and personal security that enables you to not be threatened every time someone says something. Listening requires that you actually stop what you are doing and focus on the person or group that is in front of you.

Why is listening so important?

Listening enables you to really understand your people, understand the real causes of problems, and discover when certain issues need to be discussed. Every other communication skill is useless if you cannot listen effectively. Can you help people become self-propelled if you do not know what their real needs are? Can you help people address problems and resolve conflicts if you do not understand what the real issues are? The answer is obviously no. Emphatically no! Listening is the essential communication skill.

If you learn to *really* listen, you will discover that people will tell you everything you need to know to help them be successful.

Essential skills for listening

There are six essential skills you must develop if you are going to be an effective listener. Some of these may be familiar to you but some will probably be new skills.

- Temporary selflessness – Temporary selflessness means that for the time period that you are listening, you are not concerned about you and your needs. You are instead concerned about understanding the other person's needs. In order to achieve this state of temporary selflessness, you must know your own needs and consciously set them aside. This may sound rather paradoxical, but it is in fact true. You cannot consciously set your needs or feelings aside unless you understand them. Most leaders try to deny their needs or desires rather than understand them. When you deny your needs or desires, they do not go away. Instead, they just go underground. They will then emerge whenever you feel threatened or insecure.

- Genuine caring – Genuine caring means that you find something about the person or the situation to really care about. Genuine caring does not mean that you become buddies with your people. Genuine caring simply means that you want your people to succeed personally and professionally. If you really care about the individual or group and you can temporarily forget your personal needs, you will be able to focus on them and what they need.

- <u>Emotional objectivity</u> – Many times when you listen to people their comments may cause feelings and emotions which cause you to stop listening to them. These may be frustration, anger, resentment, guilt, or related emotions. When these emotions come, you must be able to deal with them objectively and then let go of them so that you can stay focused on the individual or team and their concerns. Emotional objectivity means that you listen to what people really are saying rather than reading your emotions or feelings into their words.

- <u>Reflecting</u> – Reflecting is the skill of communicating back to the person what he has said so that both you and he know that you have really understood him. This simple skill can be a tremendous resource once you realize that your job is not to "fix" the situation all the time. Most leaders live with the mistaken notion that they should always be fixing things for their people. What your people really want is dialogue. They want conversation about work. They are usually capable of solving their own problems. Reflecting someone's thoughts lets the person know he is valued and communicates that they are "somebody."

- <u>Questioning</u> – Questioning is developing the ability to ask questions to keep the other person talking so that you can understand more detail.

- <u>Summarizing</u> – This is the ability to summarize at the end of the conversation so that you and the other person know that you have understood him and his needs.

Preparation for listening

Good listening requires preparation. Even if you are approached in the hall without much time to prepare, the following thoughts can help you be an effective listener when others approach you.

- Genuine Caring – Make sure that you are really concerned about the person's or team's success. If you are not really concerned about the person's success, you will probably not be effective at listening and coaching.
- Focus on the individual or group – Make sure that you focus on the person or the team. Most leaders live very busy lives. It is easy to fall into the mistaken belief that you can listen to people and their needs while doing paperwork or some other task. If you think you are that good, think again. While you may think you are doing a good job, the other person is clearly reading that the paperwork is more important than he is. If this is in fact the case, let the person know that you cannot talk now and that you need to reschedule a time to talk.
- Remove distractions – Remove pagers, phone, computer and any other distractions that will inhibit your listening ability.
- Remember your goal – When someone comes to you to talk, your first goal is to understand the person, his needs, and the dynamics of the situation. Why does the person want to talk with you? What is the issue? What are the dynamics of the situation? The initial goal is not to fix the problem. The initial goal is to understand. Resist the temptation to fix the problem for the person. Remember, your bigger goal is developing self-propelled people. If you are solving problems for people because that is the most convenient thing to do, you are not developing your people. Obviously, there are times when it is right to solve problems for your people. However, if people are capable of solving the problem for themselves and should be solving the problem themselves, you should resist the temptation to solve it for them.

- Know what to observe or hear - Can you imagine going to your physician with a problem and your physician not knowing what to listen for in your conversation and what to observe? He would not be your physician for long. Physicians are taught in medical school how to observe and listen to really understand what the problem is. The same must be true of effective leaders. You must know what to observe and what to listen for so that you can understand people and their needs. There are four essential items you should listen for and listen to in your conversations:
  - Word choice - What does it say about the person's beliefs or the dynamics in the situation? First listen for the actual words that are used in the conversation.
  - Tone of voice - Someone can say, "I had a great day," but it can mean different things depending on the tone of voice that the person uses. If someone really sounds excited it obviously means that the day really was great. If the tone of voice has a hint of sarcasm, then obviously it is another story.
  - Body language -What does someone's body language say to you? If someone's body language appears nervous or frustrated, you should look for an explanation or cause of such. If the person appears angry, then address what you see. Remember, if you want self-propelled people, you must help them learn how to manage their feelings and emotions. To do this you must be able to observe people's body language and be prepared to talk about what you observe.
  - Silence - Silence is a difficult experience for most leaders to endure. When silence occurs, the natural tendency is to fill the empty space with words. Resist the temptation. Wait for the other person to talk.

    A few years ago I was leading a series of internal listening sessions for a client. The group immediately after lunch was very quiet. After about five minutes of asking questions and having no response, I said, "Help me interpret the silence. You are quiet for one of four reasons:

1. You do not understand me.
2. You don't have anything to say.
3. You are asleep.
4. You do not believe it is emotionally safe to talk in this meeting.

Which one is it?" There was again silence and then some-one said, "The real truth is that we have gone through these listening sessions before and nothing has happened with our suggestions. We are not certain that it is worth talking and making suggestions again." Once I understood the reason for the silence I could address the issue.

- Know your needs - If you cannot talk when someone approaches you, say so in a pleasant way and reschedule the meeting. However, make sure that you keep the rescheduled appointment.

How to listen when others approach you

There is a logical process to listening. If you can understand and apply this process it will enhance your listening significantly.

- Understand the purpose of the conversation –
  What does the person want to discuss? Whenever someone approaches you to talk there is always a reason. The reason may be business or it may be personal. Your first responsibility is to understand the purpose of the conversation. The other person will usually define the purpose of the conversation. *"Do you have a minute where we can talk about ..."* If the other person does not define the purpose, you can simply define it with one of the following introductions, *"Hello Susan. What's up?" "How are you today? Is they're anything specific you wanted to discuss today?" "What is on your mind?"*

- Understand the motive of the person –
  The motive is the reason why the person wants to talk about the subject. The motive is usually one of six things:
  - Lack of understanding – The person needs knowledge.
  - Disagreement – The person disagrees with something that has happened.
  - Fear – The person is afraid of losing security or power or control.
  - Anger – The person is upset about a decision or action.
  - Guidance and direction – The person is seeking guidance.
  - Action – The person wants you to do something.

- Listen for information to understand details about the situation –
  - Listen to understand the basic concept or issue that the person is discussing. Many people are not good at communicating the real issue. They may dance around the issue or talk about it obliquely with the hope that you will really understand it. You may have to ask clarifying questions to gain a clear understanding of what the real issue is.
  - Listen to the tone of voice and observe body language. Tone of voice and body language will usually tell you how strong the person's feelings are. If the person exhibits behavior that tells you they are upset about the topic, it may be useful to reflect this to the person, *"This issue obviously has upset you."* If the person exhibits behavior that tells you they are confused then reflect this to the person, *"The way this was communicated to you was confusing. Am I right?"*
  - Listen for word choice. Word choice will usually tell you what the person really believes about an issue, a situation or a person. In conflict management workshops people will often use negative words when they talk about conflict. They will not even realize the words they used. When these words are brought to their attention, they will often talk about how they really feel about conflict. These negative words tell you that conflict is a negative thing for them. Until

this negativity is addressed, the person will never deal effectively with conflict.

- Clarify if you get conflicting signals –
  It is not unusual for people to send conflicting signals in a conversation. If someone is uncomfortable dealing with conflict, the person may express anger at one point and then feel guilty for expressing the anger and appear to be not upset at all. Some people will begin a conversation talking about one topic and then switch to another topic once the conversation begins. If you get conflicting signals or if you find yourself confused in the conversation, clarify this with the person. *"Bill, when you started you said you were upset. Now you say everything is fine. I am confused." "Jennifer, you started talking about yesterday's meeting and now you are talking about your frustration with the credit department. What is the real issue that concerns you?"*

- Summarize or help the person summarize –
  If the topic is work related or is causing the person frustration, it may be useful to summarize the conversation at the conclusion. If the person is upset, this can also be a way to help the person focus on what to do next. *"So if you can understand the reason for the decision, you will feel better." "It is obvious you are upset. What are you going to do to resolve the issue?" "I think that is a good decision."* The intent of summarizing is to help the person crystallize his thoughts or move further toward action.

- Determine if action is needed by the person or if the person wants action from you –
  One of the biggest dilemmas that a coach faces is deciding when to take action and when to step back and let the other person take action. Keep in mind that your goal is to develop self-propelled people. You want your people to resolve their own

problems as much as possible. Be slow to fix situations for people if they are capable of fixing them on their own. If their responsibility is to take action, coach them on what to do but help them understand that resolving the issue is their responsibility.

Action Steps

Listening is one skill that requires constant practice. Set a time each day when you will intentionally practice this skill. Review the chapter before you begin. Once your conversation is complete, review it and learn from it. If you really want to improve your listening skills, get feedback from your people. When you complete a conversation, ask the following questions:

- *"I am trying to improve my listening skills. Will you give me some honest feedback on our conversation?"*
- *"Did you think that I was really listening to you and understanding your concerns?"*
  If yes—*"What did I do that made you think I really was listening?"*
  If no—*"What did I do that made you think I was not really listening?"*
- *"What could I do to be a better listener?"*

If you decide to get feedback, make sure you do something with the feedback. Remember you may not like what you hear but it is how the other person perceives you that is important.

CHAPTER SIXTEEN

Thinking on Your Feet

*The problem most of the time is that people go
into a conversation without plan B.*

When I was a pastor, one person in the church was constantly upset with me about something. Unfortunately, I never heard it directly from the person. I always heard about it from someone else. Someone would come by my office and say, "John, Edna sure is upset about that sermon you preached yesterday," or "Edna didn't like that decision we made at church conference last week." I suggested to the person that Edna should come to me and discuss it. However, Edna never came to me. This went on for quite some time. She was not willing to come and talk to me, and I decided I wasn't going to respond unless she wanted to talk with me personally.

Finally, after a few months of hearing this I said, "Enough is enough." I called Edna and asked her if we could talk. She agreed and we planned to meet at my office the next day after she finished work. As I prepared to meet with Edna, I asked myself this question, "What do you really want to know when she comes?" What I really wanted to know was why she was upset with me all of the time. With that as my goal, I began to plan the conversation. I decided on the following introduction, "Edna, I know you have some problems with me and I would like to understand what those are to see if there are any changes that I can make." I thought that this opening might get the barriers down and open the door for dialogue.

I liked the introduction but then another thought came to mind. "What if she says that she doesn't have a problem with me?" I realized that this answer could be a distinct possibility because most people do not like conflict. If the word "problem" sounds too harsh, what could I do? I decided to rephrase the sentence using concerns if she said she did not have any problems with me.

The next hour was spent thinking through the conversation using this same approach. I thought about what I would say, and then identified the possible things she might say or do in response. With each of these possibilities, I decided on a plan of action that would keep the conversation moving toward my goal of understanding her real concerns. That afternoon, Edna came into the office and sat down. The conversation began like this:

"Edna, I know that you have some problems with me."
Edna cut in at that point and said, "John I don't have any problems with you."
"Well, I know you have some concerns."
"I do have some concerns John."
"Good, I said, "lets talk about them.

The conversation lasted about an hour. At the end of the conversation, I sensed that it had been time well spent. About eighteen months later I left the church to pursue another career. She was one of my biggest supporters. This never would have happened if I had not planned my conversation.

What I learned in planning for that conversation

Performance Coaching Principle #16

Plan your conversation. Never go into a coaching situation without anticipating problems and how to address them.

That day was one of the most valuable days in my career as a pastor and in my subsequent career as a consultant and speaker. I realized the most important principle that someone must understand and apply if he or she is to be an effective communicator and a resolver of problems: Never go into a potentially divisive conversation without plan B. Unfortunately, most leaders do not follow this advice. Most leaders plan for a conversation by thinking about how they want the conversation to go. They know in their mind what they want to say and how they want their people to react. Unfortunately, they do not plan what to do if the conversation does not go the way they want. When the leader does not develop a "plan B" he has no place to go when the conversation gets off track. The leader must either back out of the conversation or get aggressive, neither of which is a good option when discussing performance issues with your people.

The steps in using the dialogue-planning tree

Another discovery I made on that day was the dialogue-planning tree, a simple way to plan for a conversation so that you can keep the conversation focused on the goal of the conversation. There are three simple steps to using the dialogue-planning tree.

- Define the goal or desired outcome of the conversation. Before you begin any coaching conversation, you must have a clear understanding of your goal in the conversation. Why are you talking with the person? Usually, there are four potential goals in any conversation related to work:

  - To understand – Many times, your sole purpose in talking with someone is to understand his or her perspective. If this is your goal, it is important that you stay focused on understanding. Resist the temptation to start fixing things unless it is logical to do so at this time. This goal is very important if you are seeking to develop self-propelled people because you must understand how they think.

  - To be understood – At times, the reason for meeting with someone is to make sure that the person understands you. If this is your goal, remember that just because you "tell" someone something does not mean that they understand. You must ask questions and get feedback to be certain that the person understands.

  - To get commitment toward a certain action – There are times that you want people to agree to do certain things. If this is the reason for the meeting, you can plan your introduction and thought process accordingly.

  - To discuss consequences – There are times when people have to understand the consequences that will occur if they continue to do certain things. This usually is the goal after you have had numerous conversations about the topic and there has been no improvement.

- Develop your introduction.
  The introduction is the most critical part of any conversation. If the conversation begins effectively, it will move toward the goal that you desire. However, an ineffective introduction will produce an ineffective meeting or one that must be stopped and scheduled at a later date. The goal of the introduction is to begin the conversation in a way that will bring barriers down, open the

person to dialogue and move the conversation toward the goal. Another way to phrase this is, "How do I begin the discussion so that the person will open up and say what they really think or feel?" There are three steps that usually help with any introduction:

A) State the topic to be discussed

B) Use an "I" message

C) Request dialogue

"Susan, can we talk about what happened at the end of the meeting yesterday? I sensed that you were frustrated, but I was not exactly sure why you were frustrated."

- Develop plan "B."

  In every conversation, you have a mental plan for how you want the conversation to go. This is plan "A". In plan "A" you ask questions and the person responds exactly as you hope he will. You make statements and the person understands. The only problem is that most conversations do not go completely according to plan "A". To achieve your goal in the conversation you must have plan "B". Plan "B" simply means that you anticipate the things that could go wrong in the conversation and plan your response to keep the conversation on track toward your goal.

It may be useful to think of the plan "A" responses as the desired responses and the plan "B" responses as the unexpected responses. These unexpected responses may be aggressive or passive. They may be logical or emotive. The unexpected response may be silence or it may be excess verbiage. In all cases, you must (and I mean *must*) anticipate these and plan what to say, do or ask if this response comes.

Don't get lost in the conversation

The most common mistake that leaders make in coaching conversations is losing sight of the goal. The most frequent example is to shift the goal from understanding the person to fixing a problem. If your goal in the conversation is to understand the person, resist the temptation to fix the problem immediately. Many times, the person can fix the problem himself if you stay focused on understanding. The only way to resist this temptation is to be aware of the tendency and to develop plan "B" to keep you on track toward your goal.

Planning is different than manipulation

Occasionally I will have someone say, "John, if I plan for the conversation, it seems like I am really manipulating the conversation and the person. Is that true?" The answer is a resounding NO! Manipulation means that you get someone to do something that benefits you, not them. Manipulation is a very self-centered act. Planning for a conversation, on the other hand, is a very "other person focused act." Planning for a conversation means that you really want to listen and understand the other person so that the conversation can achieve a mutually beneficial ending. Using the dialogue-planning tree is really a way to keep from manipulating the conversation. If you plan for the conversation, you will not be caught off guard with something that the person says. If you are not caught off guard, you are free to really listen to the person and understand his or her need, how to solve the problem, or whatever is the goal of the conversation.

Closing Thoughts

The dialogue-planning tree provides you with a "game plan" for any conversation. You may still get caught off guard occasionally, but these occasions will be few and far between. Using the dialogue-planning tree will enable you to be more aware of your own feelings and not get distracted by them. It will enable you to really focus your energy on the other person.

Action Steps

This week there is at least one important meeting you will have. Use the dialogue-planning tree now to plan for the conversation.

CHAPTER SEVENTEEN

Questioning Skills

To understand how people think, you must ask questions.

There is a logical progress to building self-propelled people.
- First, you must understand them, both how they think and act.
- To understand people, you must listen to them.
- To listen, you must first get the other person talking. This means you must stop telling, telling, and telling all of the time.
- To get people to talk, you must ask questions.

Somehow, this simple logical process is missed by a multitude of leaders, even though it is very, very uncomplicated. To understand how your people think, they must talk, not you! If you can learn how to ask questions effectively, you will learn everything you need to know about helping your people be successful, meeting your customer's needs, and building an enduring organization.

Jerry Morgan was one of the few people I know who truly mastered the art of questioning. Jerry was the factory manager at the Wm. Wrigley Jr. Co. factory in Flowery Branch, Georgia, before his untimely death due to cancer. On more than one occasion I watched

Jerry start a conversation and move through the entire conversation by only asking questions. It was a joy to watch. Without realizing it at the time, Jerry was developing self-propelled people everyday because he was forcing them to think.

Performance Coaching Principle #17

To understand how others think, you must ask questions.

<u>*Why leaders do not use questions more*</u>

Leaders do not use the questioning process for one of three reasons:

- <u>They believe that their role is to talk or to tell people what to do.</u>
Many leaders believe that their job is to tell their people what to do. This belief limits their desire and ability to learn the questioning process, as well as their patience to use the questioning process. The questioning process takes more time in the beginning than simply telling people what to do. Telling is more convenient. The only problem with telling is that telling only breeds more telling. If you are tired of telling, maybe you should do something different. Remember, your people are not going to do something different unless you first do something different.
- <u>They are uncomfortable with the questioning process because they have never done it before.</u>
Many leaders know they should stop just telling but they really do not understand how to use questions effectively. To avoid looking stupid or making a fool of themselves, they simply keep telling.
- <u>They are afraid that this will lead to conflict.</u>
Many leaders are deathly afraid of conflict. This will be covered in detail in Chapter Nineteen, but a brief comment is warranted

here. Many people do not ask questions because they are afraid that it will lead to conflict. As a leader, you must understand that you will never develop self-propelled people (and I mean never!!!!!) until you learn to manage confrontation and conflict effectively. You do not have to like conflict but you must learn to manage it effectively.

Three types of questions

There are three types of questions that leaders use. Two of these are valid question forms. The third one should be avoided.

- Open-ended questions
  Open-ended questions require someone to explain or discuss their answer. Open-ended questions usually begin with how, why, what, or another word that implies explanation. Most of the questions that you will use when coaching your people are open-ended questions. Here are some examples: *"Susan, tell me what happened after the meeting? Why do you feel this way? What can we do to improve? How could you do things differently next time?"* Do you notice the tone of each question? They all require explanations.
- Closed-ended questions
  Closed-ended questions require a yes or no answer. Closed-ended questions should only be used when you are asking someone to take a specific action or when you want a yes or no response.
- Leading questions
  Leading questions are questions in which you try to put words in the other person's mouth. Leading questions always start with some version of, "Don't you think..." You should avoid using leading questions at all costs. When you ask a leading question, people realize that you want them to give you a certain answer. At that point they have to make a decision. Do I tell them what

I really think or do I tell them what I think they want to hear? The 80% will usually tell you what they think you want to hear. When this happens, many leaders are fooled because they think their people came up with the right answer on their own. In reality, all their people did was mimic what the leader said. This creates compliance, not self-propelled people.

The linear flow of questioning

When questioning, you will usually work in a linear fashion, from "What is the problem?" to "What is the solution?" The questions will usually flow in the following order:

Questioning flow:
What happened? *"Let's talk about what just happened."*

Questioning flow:
Why did it happen? *"Help me understand why you did this."* Or *"Why did you act this way?"* Or *"Why did you do this?"*

Questioning flow:
What was the person's intent? *"What did you hope or intend to achieve or accomplish?"*

Questioning flow:
What belief caused him to act this way? *"What was the belief that inclined you to act this way?"* Or *"Tell me what you were thinking?"*

Questioning flow:
Why does the person think this way? *"Let's talk about why you thought this was the right thing to do."*

Questioning flow:
What was the impact of this event? *"How did this affect others in the organization – teamwork, productivity, etc.?"*

Questioning flow:
What information, experience or influence does the person need to change his beliefs? *"Would it be beneficial to work with ... this week? Is there a seminar that can help you better understand what to do?"*

Questioning flow:
What needs to be done next time? *"What needs to be done the next time?" "What is the action plan that we should develop to make sure it is done the next time?"*

Questioning flow:
Will the person commit to the new behavior? *"Can I get an agreement from you to take this action next time?"*

In the example above, the goal of the questioning process was two-fold. First, the leader needed to know what really happened and why it happened. Second, the leader and the person needed to develop a plan and make a commitment to change behavior in the future.

If you examine the questions above, the easiest action would have been for the leader to tell the person what to do. However, this action would not help the person know what to do in the future. Neither does it encourage the person to take the responsibility of solving problems on his own.

Listening and questioning

The linear flow of questions just discussed provides an overall framework for question flow. In reality, the actual flow of questions and the questions used will be determined by what the other person says. If you are listening effectively, the other person's actions and words will lead you naturally to the next question. Having the linear flow of questions in your head will help you by providing a general road map for your conversation. For example, if you are in the middle of the conversation and you suddenly see that the person's mood has shifted, you will want to ask a question to examine why his mood has changed before moving forward in your linear flow. If you do not ask this question, you may miss a valuable insight that can help you develop this person into a self-propelled person.

Move from general questions to specific questions

When asking questions, it is also useful to move from the general to the specific. This means that the opening question will be something like, *"Tell me what happened,"* or *"Explain the steps you took to do this."* From that question, the following questions should be more specific, based on the information that you receive from the other person.

Planning the questioning process

When you first begin using the questioning process, it will be useful for you to take a few minutes to plan for questioning. It may even be useful in the early stages of learning to write down your questions and your thoughts. The dialogue-planning tree in Chapter Sixteen can assist you at this point. The process of writing them down will usually reinforce the questioning process. The following steps can help you in the planning process:

- Identify your goal in questioning.
  Why are you using questions in this conversation? Usually you
  will use questions for one of the following reasons:
  - A) You need to understand the other person.
  - B) You want the other person to explain themselves.
  - C) You want the person to commit to a certain action.

- Understand what is important to the other person.
  What motivates him? What is his reason for working? Is he
  working because he loves his career or is he working because
  he has to pay the bills? What are his goals and dreams? If you
  know what is important to the person, you can better plan your
  questions and how to help the person be successful. There are
  two areas about which you should be concerned:
  - What is important to the person in general? What are the
    things that he values? What is important in his personal life?
  - What is important to the person at work? If you know what
    is important to the person at work it can help you ask the
    right questions to help the person become self-propelled.

- Identify how your goal in the conversation and the person's goals
  relate.
  When you can connect these two, you create an environment
  for the person to excel and for your organization to naturally
  succeed. You should be able to answer these two questions:
  - How can achieving their goal (Step two) help you achieve
    your goal (in the conversation - step one)?
  - How can achieving your goal (step one) help them achieve
    their goals (step two)?

- Plan your introduction.
  The first thirty seconds of any conversation are the most critical. The introduction of any conversation should accomplish three important things:
  - Clearly communicate the issue to be discussed
  - Pull the barriers down
  - Create a safe environment for dialogue

  Whenever you begin an important conversation, take a few minutes to plan the introduction. Even if you are not initiating the conversation, plan what you want to know in the introduction. This will enable you to ask questions from the start if the other person is not clear in beginning the conversation.

- Anticipate problems.
  The Dialogue-Planning Tree in Chapter Sixteen is designed to help you anticipate problems that may occur in the conversation. It is always wise when planning the questioning process to anticipate problems that may occur. This will give you time to think about questions you can ask should the conversation not go as you anticipated.

- Be aware of your "emotional hooks" that will cause you to lose objectivity in the conversation.
  Emotional hooks are the things that people say or do that cause you to lose objectivity and become biased in your conversation. For example, many leaders who are themselves self-starters get frustrated when someone makes excuses and blames others for their problems. At this point, the leader is no longer objective and will naturally want to tell the person what to do to "straighten them out." Neither of these actions will lead to self-propelled people. If someone is constantly blaming others, the leader must discover the pattern and address the pattern in the following manner: *"Mike, have you ever noticed that you have a tendency to blame others when you are not successful? You do*

not appear to be willing to identify and focus on the things within your control that can help you be successful." A response like this will more likely move the person closer to becoming self-propelled than if you get frustrated and "read them the riot act."

- Develop a standard set of questions for common situations. Even though every conversation with people will be unique, patterns emerge in these conversations. If you desire to stay focused in your conversations, it may be helpful to identify common problems or situations that occur and develop a standard set of questions to use in such situations. Below are four common situations and possible questions to use in each situation.

Situation: Person is trying to sidetrack the conversation or change the subject.
Question: *"Betty, why are we talking about this?"*

Situation: Person avoids answering question.
Question: *"Tommy, why are you avoiding answering the question?"*

Situation: Person is quiet.
Question: *"Bill, tell me why you are suddenly silent?"*

Situation: Person becomes visibly upset.
Question: *"Patty, why is this so upsetting to you?"* *"What is it about this conversation that is upsetting to you?"*

Situation: Person gets aggressive.
Question: *"Alan, tell me why you are suddenly ...(describe the aggressive behavior that you see.)"*

Using the questioning process to get commitment

One area where questioning is extremely valuable is in getting commitment. Many leaders still fall prey to the trap of telling people what to do and thinking that they are getting commitment from the person. To use the questioning approach to get commitment, try the following:

- First, ask questions to understand the other person.
- Second, ask questions to make sure that the other person understands what needs to be done.
- Next, ask for commitment. This is usually done with a closed ended question. This is one of the important times to use a closed-ended question. Below are some of the questions that can be used when asking for commitment.

   "Are you willing to do this...?"
   "Would you be willing to try this for the next week?"
   "Can I get your commitment to do this in the future?"
   "Do you understand that this is your responsibility?"
   "What are you going to do then when this situation occurs in the future?"
- Finally, set a time for follow-up.

Using the questioning process when people approach you about the appropriate action to take

The temptation to "tell, tell, tell" is most prevalent when someone approaches you about what to do in a given situation. If you think that the person really knows what needs to be done or has a good idea of what needs to be done, consider the following approach:

- The person approaches you and says, "What should I do?" If he is experienced to the point that he has an idea about the corrective action to take, resist the temptation to just tell him.

- Ask him, "What do you think should be done?" The purpose of asking him is twofold: First, to see what his answer will be, and second, to explore his thinking so that you know he has the correct thought process. If he has no answer, restate the question in a less threatening form so that he will be encouraged to speculate about the right answer.

- Ask him, "Why do you think this is the correct thing to do?" Even if he tells you the right action to take, still ask the question. This step is designed for you and the person to examine his thought process. If he is thinking correctly, you want to affirm his thought process. There are occasions where he will know the right thing to do in this situation but he will not know why it is the right thing to do. Without this second level of knowledge, he may not make the right decision if some of the factors change in the future. If he selects the incorrect action, you want to help examine his thinking so that in the future he can develop the correct action.

- Ask him, "Are you comfortable taking this action?" Ask the person if he is comfortable taking the action discussed above. If he is, have him take the appropriate action now. If he is uncomfortable taking the action now, examine why.

What happens if the situation occurs again? If the problem occurs a second time, follow the above steps again. If it occurs a third time begin by asking the question, *"Is the situation the same as before?"* If the answer is no, then review the above steps. If the answer is yes, then ask the following question: *"If you were comfortable taking the appropriate action in the past, why are you not comfortable taking action now?"*

Actions Steps

- Identify a coaching situation that you will or should have with one of your people in the next thirty days.
- Develop a plan for this conversation that is predominantly focused on asking questions.
- Practice a "telling-free" dialogue. In the workshops that we lead, one exercise that we do is a role-play where the leader can only ask questions to resolve or address a situation. Try the same exercise yourself.
- Make a commitment every day for the next week to engage in one conversation where you only use questions. Choose a non-work related situation at first. This will let you get comfortable with the process in a non-threatening setting. Once you have practiced it a few times, select a simple work-related conversation to practice using questioning. Plan your question flow the first few times you do it. The dialogue-planning tree can assist you.

CHAPTER EIGHTEEN

Speaking The Truth with Compassion

Sometimes the truth is the hardest thing to say.

The problem of honesty in the workplace

People are often uncomfortable saying what they really want to say. This situation occurs at every level of organizations throughout the world. People know what they want to say but something keeps them from really saying it. To develop self-propelled people, it is imperative that you communicate in an honest and caring way regarding their performance. If you are not honest with your people, they cannot grow and improve. If you "sugarcoat" your words so that situations seem OK, people cruise along thinking everything is great when in fact it is not. If you are honest, but do so in a cold and hateful way, they will either give up or see you as the real cause of their problems. In all of these situations, you are not developing self-propelled people.

Always keep your goal in front of you. Your goal is to develop self-propelled people. Remember Performance Coaching Principle #2? If you want people to do something different, you have to do something different. One of the things you must do differently is learn to speak the truth in a caring way.

Definition of speaking the truth with compassion

Performance Coaching Principle #18

To help people improve, you must speak the truth in a caring way.

Speaking the Truth with Compassion means developing the ability to communicate what you think or feel about an issue in a way that lets the other person know that you care about him, the organization and the issue. The goal of speaking the truth with compassion is accurate communication done in a caring way.

Why leaders don't speak the truth

There are three primary reasons that people do not speak the truth with compassion:

- Fear of conflict – Most people, including leaders, find conflict very uncomfortable. Because of this personal uneasiness with conflict there is a tendency to avoid situations that will potentially lead to conflict. This is discussed in detail in the next chapter.

- Politics in the organization – I was recently working with a client that had a new division leader in the organization. I was talking with one of the middle managers about how things were going. The person said, "Meetings are just a waste of time now. No one really talks at meetings any more. Everyone waits to see what the new leader thinks and then they all line up behind him". My friend's comments were a classic example of how politics can get in the way of speaking the truth with compassion. The new leader wanted to get things started in a positive way and was well received in the organization. In response, the other leaders in the organization quickly thought they had to "line up" behind the new leader if they wanted to "get ahead." Valuable information may be lost when people "jockey for position" rather than honestly address the issues.
- Lack of Training – For many leaders, the real issue is that they do not really know how to speak the truth with compassion, because they have never been taught how to do it.

Why speaking the truth with compassion is so important in your organization

Speaking the truth with compassion is a critical skill for you to learn as a coach. Without it, you will be hampered in your process to build self-propelled people. But speaking the truth with compassion is bigger and more important than just helping develop self-propelled people. Today's busy work environment requires that everyone use his or her head, hands and feet to help the organization be successful. If this is not being done and is not being addressed, the organization will suffer.

Speaking the truth with compassion is also a sign that you genuinely care for your people and the organization's success. I confess that in most situations I am more of a pragmatist than an idealist. On this point, though, I am an unashamed idealist. If you genuinely care for your people, it is critical that you be honest with them in a caring way. You must learn how to give them feedback in a way that helps them grow and develop. Speaking the truth with compassion is the only way to do this.

Think from their perspective not yours

If the issues that you address with someone are positive, you will naturally speak the truth in a caring way. The problem comes when you must discuss a difficult, uncomfortable or potentially volatile issue with someone. One thing that can help you speak the truth with compassion is to think about the situation from the other person's perspective, not just from your perspective. If you "put yourself in his or her shoes" you may gain understanding that can help you speak the truth in a way that others will hear it and understand.

Most people have good intentions. Unfortunately, what actually happens may not be consistent with the intent. Speaking the truth with compassion is easier if you assume the intent of the person is good instead of assuming the worst. Usually, the problem lies in the execution of the intent and not the intent itself.

Actions that can help you speak the truth with compassion

While speaking the truth with compassion may not be easy for many leaders, there are some actions that you can take to make it easier.

- Develop communication guidelines.
  One of the best things you can do to open communication is to establish ground rules or guidelines for communication and to reinforce these. Developing guidelines is very simple.

- – Identify the major characteristics you wish to see in the communication in your area.
- – Make sure that these will encourage communication to be positive and goal focused.
- – Develop guidelines based on these characteristics.
- – Get a commitment from the team to use these guidelines to guide communication.
- – Periodically review these to make sure that people are using them.
- – If the guidelines are violated, immediately address this.
- Structure regular meetings for the person or team to evaluate progress.

  Planned follow-up sessions are one of the best actions to help you speak the truth with compassion. Regular times of meeting to discuss performance opens the door for honest communication to help the person improve.

- Develop a method to quickly address problems when they occur.

  It is best to develop an agreeable method for quickly addressing problems before the problems occur. When the person is in a non-threatening setting, discuss how he wants to have problems addressed should they occur in the future. Once you and the person have discussed this, both of you commit to use this process. Should problems occur in the future, simply let the person know that you are going to use the process that was agreed upon. Example: "You said that if there was a problem you wanted me to come directly to you. There is something that we need to discuss."

- Ask relevant questions and listen to what your people are saying.

Surface issues and the real issue

Most conversations about performance or problem solving involve two types of issues: surface issues and the real underlying issues. If you are to speak the truth with compassion, you must learn to distinguish between surface issues and real issues. Surface issues are the circumstances, the observable behaviors or the actions that are the reason you are talking with the person. Real issues are the underlying issues that led to or caused the surface issues. Usually the underlying issues relate to beliefs that the person has about himself, his role, the organization, system problems in the organization, lack of skills, or lack of consistent reinforcement.

Leaders often have a tendency to focus on the surface issues and not on the core issues. If you want to develop self-propelled people, you must learn how to recognize and then address the core issues. The only way that the surface issues will be improved or resolved is to address the underlying issues.

- Here is a simple example. Patty is late for work on a regular basis. This is a source of frustration for you and the other people in the organization. Most leaders simply talk with Patty about being on time in the future. At the end of this conversation Patty says that she will try harder to be on time in the future. Patty is on time for a short period of time. Eventually, she falls back into her old patterns. Eventually you will have the same conversation with her – perhaps many times. The problem never really gets resolved.

  If you are addressing the underlying issues then you would chose a different approach. First you would examine her performance over time, looking for patterns. Something is getting in the way of Patty being on time. You might then say something like one of the following: _"Patty either getting to work on time is not a high priority to you or you are not managing your time well_ *in the morning. Which one is it?"* Or *"Patty, during the last month you have been late for work eight times. It appears to me that being on time for work is not a high priority for you. Am I right?"* Or *"Patty, it seems to me that you think it is OK to be late for work as long as you get your work done by the end of the day. Am I right?"* In all of these cases, the attempt is to address the underlying issue. If the underlying issue is addressed, she will usually change her behavior or recognize that she does not fit into the culture at your organization.

Steps to speaking the truth with compassion

The following steps can help you learn how to speak the truth with compassion to your people.

- Invest in the relationship.

  You must make an investment of time, energy and emotion in the relationship. Without this, anything you say related to problems or conflicts will be perceived as uncaring.

- Define the goal of the conversation.

  What do I want to accomplish in this interaction with the person? Usually the goal of the conversation is one of four things:
  - To understand the other person
  - To have the other person understand you
  - To get the other person to commit to a certain action
  - To help the other person understand consequences

- Understand yourself and the other person.

  It is important for you to understand your own behavior patterns and the behavior patterns of the people in your organization. One resource that can assist you is a behavior profile. There are a number of them on the market today. We use the Personal Profile System by Inscape Publishing. This profile is known as the DISC behavior profile. The value of using a behavior profile is that it enables you to discuss behavior in objective terms. For information on behavior profiles call us at 706-795-3557.

- Assess the risk level.

Many people do not speak the truth with compassion because they are afraid. Before you speak the truth with compassion, take an honest assessment of the risks by answering these questions:

What fear is keeping you from speaking the truth with compassion?

What things do you fear losing?

What is the worst thing that could happen if you speak the truth with compassion?

What could you gain by speaking the truth with compassion?

Do the potential gains outweigh the potential negative impacts?

Under assessing risks, one should also decide if this issue is really important enough to address. If it affects the productivity or morale of the group, the answer is yes.

- Develop skills.

To speak the truth with compassion, you must be prepared. You must know what you want to say. You must also be observant enough to know when to ask questions and explore the person's mood changes. Use the dialogue-planning tree to anticipate the dialogue.

- Practice how to listen so that you can really hear what the other person is saying.

Practice the skills you learned in Chapter Fifteen, "Listening," so you can really under stand what others are saying.

- Effective speaking involves effective listening.

You must be able to observe the person's body language and hear when their tone of voice changes. Here are some things that can help you listen better:

Know your thoughts and feelings and their source.

Anticipate the dialogue.

Set a time to talk and communicate that this is an important meeting.

Begin by using an "I" message.
Try getting a commitment to resolve the problem at the beginning of the dialogue.
When you get uncomfortable, say so.
Plan follow-up after the meeting.

Action Step

Identify a situation in which you really need to talk honestly with someone. Using the steps identified in this chapter, plan for the conversation with an emphasis on speaking the truth with compassion.

CHAPTER NINETEEN

Addressing and Resolving Conflict

*The paradox of effective conflict resolution:
To eliminate conflict, you must learn to embrace conflict.*

At some point on the journey to building self-propelled people, every leader will encounter conflict. **It is inevitable. It is unavoidable!** Your task as a leader is to learn how to manage conflict in a quick, healthy and productive way. Each of these three adjectives deserves some definition.

- Quick – Joyce Scoggins is a friend who was for many years a supervisor for the Wm. Wrigley Jr. Co. I had the joy of working with Joyce for a few years as a consultant. Joyce was fond of saying, "John, if we talk about it today, it is a conversation. If we wait a few days to talk about it or a few weeks, it is a conflict." Joyce understood the essence of "quick." If you address a problem or conflict soon after it occurs, dialogue and resolution are much easier. If you procrastinate for more than a day, however, the conflict begins to fester and grow in people's minds. "The sooner the better" is a good rule of thumb when it comes to resolving conflicts.

- Healthy – How the conflict is resolved is as important as when it is resolved. The process used must encourage honesty and straightforwardness. It must focus on the issue not the person, and must show genuine heartfelt care for the individual, the situation, and your organization. Any method that uses manipulation, coercion, control, or intimidation will not foster healthy conflict resolution. Remember, the goal is to develop self-propelled people. Manipulation, coercion, control, and intimidation create compliance and fear. Compliance and fear do not create self-propelled people.

- Productive – In the end, the conflict must really be resolved. Unresolved conflict will continue to fester and grow.

The key is what you believe

The real key to resolving conflict effectively is what you believe about conflict. If you are afraid of conflict or if you believe conflict is an evil to be avoided, you will not be effective at resolving conflict. All of the training in the world will be basically useless until you change how you think about conflict. If you believe that conflict is an enemy to be conquered or a competition to be won, you will always dominate conflict using whatever methods are necessary to win. Now is the time to ask yourself the hard question: What do you really believe, feel or think about conflict?

In truth, conflict is simply a disagreement between persons over goals, beliefs or values, methods, or timelines. Think about the last conflict that you had. What was the cause of the conflict? Usually, it was one of these issues.

Treating conflict as a disagreement can help you begin to improve your conflict resolution ability because it shifts the focus off of you and the person onto the issue that is in conflict.

The paradox of eliminating conflict

Performance Coaching Principle #19

To eliminate conflict you must learn to embrace conflict.

Most leaders would love to eliminate unhealthy conflict in their workplace. Some conflict in the organization can be healthy and helpful to the organization's growth. This conflict should be encouraged. What leaders really want to eliminate is the unhealthy and unnecessary conflict that drags people and the organization down, because the morale and productivity of your organization are influenced by such conflict.

If you want to eliminate conflict you must understand what we call the paradox of no more conflict: To eliminate conflict you must learn to embrace conflict. Much conflict occurs because people are afraid to address it, and they postpone addressing it until it is a full-blown conflict. If leaders can overcome their fear of conflict or their need to "win" at conflict, they can learn to address it in a healthy way. Many conflicts can be eliminated before they occur.

Preventing Conflicts

The first step in effectively resolving conflict is to understand what you can do to eliminate conflicts before they occur. If you eliminate the conflicts before they occur, you save everyone the frustration, pain and loss of productivity usually associated with conflict. Here are some simple things that you can do to prevent conflicts:

- Know your goals and expectations and communicate them to everyone.
  The first aide in preventing conflict is to have a clear understanding of the goal to be accomplished and communicating that goal to everyone in the organization. When everyone understands the goal they are more likely to be proactive and focused in the right direction.

- Create an emotionally safe environment.
  Building self-propelled people who cooperate with one another requires that you have an emotionally safe work environment. An emotionally safe work environment is one in which people feel safe to talk about the issues affecting their ability to be effective and successful in their job. These issues may be system issues, product issues, communication issues, conflict issues, and customer or supplier issues.
  Whatever the issue, in an emotionally safe work environment people understand that it is a part of their responsibility to address issues that get in the way of their effectiveness.

  The following thoughts can assist you in developing an emotionally safe work environment:
  - Clearly define the mission, vision and values of the organization.
  - Develop *Performance goals* and *Behavioral goals* for everyone.
  - Define roles and expectations clearly for everyone.

–   Develop a mechanism for leaders to give feedback to their people and for the people to give input and feedback to the leader.
–   Establish time each week to be with your people to listen to them and their needs.
–   Develop strategies to resolve concerns when they arise. If the concern is within the control of the person then you should help the person prepare to resolve it. If the issue is outside of the control of the person, then you must be willing to do what is within your control to address the issue.
–   Develop a mechanism or process so that people know their input is being used to improve the organization.
–   Finally, ask your people what things could be done to make the organization a more emotionally safe work culture? You may be surprised at what your people say.

General guidelines for resolving conflicts

No matter how hard you try, some conflict just cannot be avoided. When this occurs, you must be prepared to effectively address the conflict in a way that truly resolves the issues. Here are some general guidelines that may assist you as you prepare to resolve conflict:

*   Genuinely care about your people -
    The first step is to genuinely care for your people and their professional and personal growth. When your people sense that you genuinely care about them, they tend to respond to you differently.
*   Be objective -
    It is critical that you remain as objective as possible when resolving conflicts. The biggest problem hindering resolution of conflict is allowing someone's word or action to influence or affect your emotion and prevent you from resolving conflict objectively.

- Use a predictable method -
  Whether you use the method of conflict resolution described in this book or one from another source, simply using a predictable method will help you to more effectively resolve conflict. If you use a predictable method, and everyone else becomes accustomed to this pattern of resolution, it increases efficiency.

- Give options when you can -
  Another help aide in resolving conflict is to give people options whenever possible. In many cases giving an option may not work, but it is worth trying whenever possible.

- Treat every conflict as a learning experience -
  What can you learn from this? Throw the whips and chains away when it comes to learning how to deal with conflict effectively. Everyone that is good at resolving conflict must learn how to do it. This means that everyone who is presently good at it was not good at some time in the past. The only way to become effective is to practice, learn from your mistakes, practice, learn from your mistakes, and keep following the repetition.

- Remember that you are responsible to the person and group, not for them -
  You are responsible for creating a work culture that makes people want to be successful, enjoy their work and be productive. You are not responsible for their success. That is ultimately their responsibility. You must simply do everything within your control to the best of your ability. This knowledge may help you stay more objective in dealing with your people and conflict.

- Do not assume malicious intent -
  Most people have good intentions in their actions. Unfortunately, how people are perceived may not be consistent with their intent. If you can keep this in mind, it may help you stay more objective and resolve the conflict sooner.

- Recognize what is in your control and what is in the control of the person or group -
  The tendency for most people is to focus their energy on things that are outside of their control. When this happens, people fall

into a pattern of griping and complaining. To effectively resolve conflict, it is essential that you understand what is within your control and what is outside of your control. Focus on the things that you can control. It will significantly enhance your success as a coach.

The five steps in resolving conflict

There are five steps to effectively resolving conflict. These five steps are identified by the acronym RADAR.

R – Recognize that the conflict exists
A – Acknowledge the conflict to the right person
D – Diagnose the conflict
A – Agree to resolve the conflict
R – Resolve the conflict

R - Recognize that the conflict exists - Many people never address conflicts because they do not admit they exist. Recognizing a conflict means that you become aware when something is not right about your relationship with a person or a group of people. Recognition is both an emotional and a mental state. During this step you will do a preliminary analysis of the conflict and develop an action plan.

Before talking with someone, do a simple analysis to identify what the conflict really is and why you think the conflict exists. If you talk with the person immediately after you recognize that there is a conflict, this analysis will be very brief and in your head. If you have time before you talk to the person, you may be able to use the process which follows to think through the conflict more thoroughly.

Once you have done a brief analysis of the conflict you must also develop a plan of action. The dialogue-planning tree in Chapter Sixteen can assist you in developing a plan for discussing the conflict.

A - <u>**Acknowledge that the conflict exists**</u> - Acknowledging the conflict means communicating to the right person that there is a problem. Acknowledging the conflict properly involves three components:

- Use an "I" message
- State the conflict to be addressed
- Request dialogue

If you use this template you can easily and quickly begin discussing the conflict. The intent of the template of "I" message, state the conflict and request dialogue" is to provide a simple and caring way to encourage dialogue. The "I" message avoids accusing the other person. Stating the conflict to be addressed lets the person know exactly what you want to discuss. The request for dialogue communicates that you want to discuss it, not control or manipulate.

D - <u>**Diagnose the conflict**</u> - Before you can resolve the conflict, you have to step back and understand why the conflict is occurring. Conflict occurs for many reasons - misunderstandings, differing goals or methods, power and control struggles, different values or beliefs. It is important that the persons involved in the conflict diagnose the conflict together. Effectively diagnosing the conflict means that all parties agree that there is a problem, clearly define the problem in objective terms, identify causes and identify how the conflict is affecting the related parties.

The following steps can help everyone more effectively diagnose the conflict.

- Define the conflict
  Clearly define the conflict or problem in objective terms. This will remove the tendency for you or the other person to take it personally.

- <u>Compare problem behavior with goal behavior</u>
  How is the conflict or problem behavior different than the desired behavior?

- <u>Analyze the conflict for patterns</u>
  Look for patterns related to conflict or problem - location, time, and people.

- <u>Identify the impact of the conflict</u>
  How is the behavior affecting morale and productivity in the organization?
  How serious is the conflict or problem?
  Has the problem been addressed before with this person?

- <u>Identify the cause or causes</u>
  Why does the problem behavior exist?
  How am I a part of the problem?
  How is the system or our leader a part of the problem?
  How is the person(s) contributing to the problem?
  Are there environmental issues?
  Are there skills and knowledge issues?
  Are there differences between goals, values and methods?
  Are there personal issues?

- <u>What beliefs are contributing to the conflict</u>
  What does the person believe about themselves, their role, the other persons involved, the organization, and the world in general that may be producing this behavior?

- <u>What is the outcome desired</u>
  What is the outcome that you desire related to this conflict or problem?

A - **Agree to resolve the conflict** - While all steps in the process are important, this is perhaps the most important. If all parties agree to resolve the conflict in a way that is acceptable to all, successful resolution is virtually insured. There must be a verbal agreement to resolve the conflict. This means that all parties must agree to stay with the conflict resolution process until a mutually agreeable solution is worked out or leaders are requested to help the persons resolve the conflict.

R - **Resolve the conflict** - For the resolution to be successful, the conflict must be resolved in a way that is agreeable to everyone, and that values and respects the personhood and needs of each person. Positive resolution should also include follow-up plans to make sure that the conflict stays resolved. If you are working in a team environment it is important for team members to attempt to resolve the conflict before you become involved. If the members of the team cannot resolve the conflict between themselves, their leader will need to become involved in the resolution process. The first attempt for conflict resolution, however, should always be between the persons with whom the conflict exists.

If all of the steps have been completed prior to this, the participants must then look for solutions that will be mutually beneficial to all. Once resolutions have been reached, the participants should also establish a "follow-up" plan to make sure that the conflicts do not reoccur or that they can be quickly addressed and resolved should they occur again.

Action Step

<u>Identifying your conflict patterns</u>

It can be helpful to identify how you usually act and react to conflict. If you are in touch with your tendencies toward conflict, you will be much more effective at addressing it.

CHAPTER TWENTY

How to Talk so that Others Will Listen

What you say and how you say it are important. Your words can inspire people to higher levels of performance or they can pierce people to the core of their being.

How to talk so that others will listen

As a leader, you should listen more than you talk. If you do listen more than you talk, you will usually be more respected when you talk. There are times, though, when you must speak. It is imperative that you learn how to talk so that people will really listen to you. Remember, talking is the easy part. Getting people to really listen and understand is a much harder task.

- The first rule of effective communication – your words and actions must be consistent.

  People look at what you do first, then they listen to what you say. If your words and your actions are not consistent, people always believe your actions. This knowledge has been around for quite a while, but many of our leaders still don't understand the concept. They espouse all of the virtues of cooperation and getting people involved in the decision making process and then they turn around and make unilateral decisions that directly impact others. As a coach, you must make sure that your words and your actions are consistent. If they are not, you are doomed!

In the Chapter One you identified the type of people you want in your organization. In Chapter Three we also discussed that most people do not have all of these characteristics that you seek. We also discussed that your responsibility is to help them develop these skills and behaviors. The example you set and how you communicate with your people will be a major key to help your people develop the skills, knowledge and beliefs that you desire.

As a coach, here are some actions that will communicate that you really care about your people and their success. If you do these things, people will pay attention to your words.

– Be with your people on a regular basis.
– Say hello to everyone during the early part of the workday.
– Vary your patterns to interact with a variety of persons.
– Talk to everyone, not just your favorites.
– Work along side your people periodically- particularly during difficult times of the day.
– Ask about the things that are important to the person.
– Provide quick feedback when you want to reinforce positive behavior.
– Provide quick feedback when you want to correct problem behavior.
– Look people in the eye.
– Smile often.
– Occasionally relieve people.

- Give recognition when someone does a good job.
- Be specific when you are communicating what needs to be done different.

Sometimes the key to consistency is avoiding certain actions. Here are some actions to avoid as a coach:

- Do not pick favorites, people will notice it.
- Do not use people as a negative example: "Let me tell you what I don't want you to do. Don't be like Janet."
- Do not make fun of someone in front of their peers or your peers: "Bill is the stupidest person I have seen in a long time."
- Do not make yourself feel better by putting someone else down.

- The second rule of effective communication – the words you use are important.

Once your actions are consistent with a coaching style of leadership, then you must focus on the words you use if you want people to listen. Words are very powerful. In many cases they can almost take on a "life of their own." Here are the types of words that you should be using as a coach.

Words that encourage people to do their best –
   "You can." "I believe in you." "You are capable."

Words that encourage people to try –
   "What is keeping you from trying this?"
   "Let's try this today and then evaluate if it is effective at the end of the day."
   "What is the worst thing that could happen?"
   "What could you gain if you did this another way?"
   "How would this affect our customers?"

Clear communication –
For communication to be effective you must use words that are clear and that the people can understand. People must understand what you are expecting and how you want them to do it.

"Susan, lets review the order in which these projects need to be done."

"Mark, the Wilson report needs to be done in Times New Roman font."

"Patty, the way you organize the workflow each day is an asset to our organization."

Make specific suggestions when improvements need to be made–
One of the mistakes leaders make when addressing problems is not being specific regarding expectations. To help people be successful, your words must be specific.

"Bill, this needs to be done every hour."

Words that respect the personhood of the person –

"I know that your intention was good, but it did not turn out as expected."

"I am not criticizing you as a person, I am saying that what you did was not right."

"You do many things very well. (List these.) To be successful, you must improve in this... area."

When mistakes are made sit down with the person and help the person learn from the mistakes –

"What happened?" "What was your intent?" "How could it be done differently the next time?"

As a coach, there are some words that you should remove from your vocabulary. These are words that discourage, demean and intimidate people. In the "old school, authoritarian style of leadership," demeaning and belittling people was an acceptable leadership style. It was OK to make someone feel worthless if he worked harder as a result. The end justified the means.

The truth is, though, that even in years gone by that style was only a short term motivator. Today, this style of leadership just does not cut it. Some people still use it, but it is as archaic as a rotary dial telephone in today's world. It does not build self-propelled people. It does not build initiative. It does not build commitment. Here are some of the key words to avoid or stop using:

The word "never" –
> *"You will never get this right." "You will never amount to anything."*

Words that belittle, discourage or demean others –
> *"How did you get this stupid?"*
> *"You are the worst employee I have ever seen."*
> *"I can't believe that you graduated from technical school."*
> *"You call this … a good job?"*
> *"You are hopeless."*

Words that imply someone is stupid or make someone feel inferior –
> *"You are slower than Christmas."*
> *"Did you really finish high school?"*
> *"I could get better results by using a group of eighth graders."*
> *"Duuuhh! Wake up Gina. Is there anything between your ears?"*

Words that compare one employee to another employee –
> *"If only all of you could be like Betty."*
> *"Betty can get this done in an hour, why can't the rest of you?"*

"I have one person that does a good job. The rest of you are worthless."

Words that put people down -
"You are a waste."
"You will never amount to anything."

Improper jokes or laughing at someone -

- The third rule of effective communication - how you say it is as important as what you say.

Sometimes we use the right words, but our tone of voice and body language communicate something very different than what we say. Here is an example. Someone can say, "Boy, I am having a great day." You will determine if they really mean what they say based on their tone of voice and body language. If their tone of voice and body language show genuine excitement, then you will believe that they truly are having a great day. If, though, their tone of voice is sarcastic, they roll their eyes and they cross their hands in disgust, then you will assume that they really have had a bad day.

It is important that you are aware of your body language and tone of voice. They will significantly impact your ability to communicate effectively.

Action Step

Meet with your leader, a mentor or a peer who will give you accurate feedback on your communication. Ask them the following questions:

What does my normal tone of voice and body language communicate to others?

Do my word choices and my actions encourage people to become self-propelled and self-motivated or do they encourage people to be dependent on me?

What can I change about my communication that will make me a more effective coach to my people?

Section III
Performance Coaching Principles

Performance Coaching Principle #12
To develop self-propelled people, you must learn to think strategically.

Performance Coaching Principle #13
The Alignment Principle - For you to achieve maximum success, how you do things must be consistent with your beliefs and goals.

Performance Coaching Principle #14
Breakdown Analysis – To help people improve, you must be able to identify the specific actions or beliefs that need to be changed.

Performance Coaching Principle #15
Listening - caring enough about an individual or group to really understand them and their needs.

Performance Coaching Principle #16
Plan your conversation. Never go into a coaching situation without anticipating problems and how to address them.

Performance Coaching Principle #17
To understand how others think, you must ask questions.

Performance Coaching Principle #18
To help people improve, you must speak the truth in a caring way.

Performance Coaching Principle #19
To eliminate conflict you must learn to embrace

Epilogue

Every leader wants self-propelled people. Every organization needs self-propelled people. We hope that this book has given you new resources and insights into developing your people into the type of self-propelled people that you desire.

As a leader you have one of the most exciting and rewarding jobs in the world. You have the opportunity to help a group of people work together to achieve goals and dreams that are greater than any one person could achieve. If your organization is going to achieve these goals and dreams, every person must do his or her part. Your job as a leader is to be the catalyst that makes this happen. We hope that the thoughts and ideas in this book will bring you one step closer to making your organization's goals and dreams a reality.

For More Information
&
Resources

For more information about JTB Communications, Inc. resources and materials contact us at 706-795-3557.

Email address:
jtbcommunications@alltel.net

Mailing Address:
John Brantley
JTB Communications, Inc.
P.O. Box 378
Danielsville, GA 30633

Ask about our bulk order discounts and non-profit discounts.

Performance Coaching – Skills Based Stratagies

If you were energized by the book *Performance Coaching – Skills Based Strategies to Develop Self Propelled People,* then we have the Performance Coaching complete training kit to accompany the book. This is a must for every organization wanting to equip leaders to guide their company to the next level.

Performance Coaching Training Kit comes complete with:
>A copy of *Performance Coaching* the book
>Participant workbook
>Participant Study Guide
>Facilitator / Trainer notes and strategies
>Audio CD's

Changing Their Script – The New Frontier for Leadership

If you have learned the essentials of performance coaching in the book *Performance Coaching – Skills Based Strategies to Develop Self Propelled People,* then you are ready to learn the most advanced leadership skills available!

Changing Their Script – The New Frontier for Leadership will teach you how to quickly align people's beliefs with your organization's beliefs to create exponential performance improvement! This tool shows you how to understand what really drives your business. Find out how to understand and tap into your employees' beliefs to help them and your organization achieve greatness!

Changing Their Script – The New Frontier for Leadership includes:
>Participant workbook
>Trainer / Facilitator guide
>Audio CD's

High Octane Teamwork

The ultimate Teamwork tool!

Teamwork is essential for high performance in every organization. *High Octane Teamwork* is an easy to follow process to help you build a high performance team!

High Octane Teamwork comes complete with:
Participant workbook
Trainer / Facilitator notes and strategies
Audio CD's
A team member pocket guide
A copy of the new business novel *High Octane Teamwork – A Trevor Benson Novel*.

Trevor Benson – A Business Novel Series

Trevor Benson, the main character in the new *Trevor Benson – A Business Novel Series*, learns the many great lessons that it takes to be a great leader from a long time friend and former CEO of a Fortune 500 company, Gus. These fast reading business novels are captivating audiences and leaving them wanting more. Call today to begin following Trevor Benson through his journey of becoming the leader that every organization wants.

TIP – Technology Improving Performance

Performance appraisal and reviews should be simple. The performance appraisal and review process is the best tool that you have to develop and coach your staff. TIP can help you make this process easy and more effective.

TIP is a very user-friendly software system built on two pillars:

- *Clear expectations and goals*
    o   Create clear expectations & job descriptions.
    o   Weighted value for each expectation.
    o   Clarify how the expectations are measured.
    o   Define the key behaviors that lead to success.
    o   Distinguish between success and outstanding performance.
- *Customized review forms for each position*
    o   Create customized performance review forms for each position.
    o   Eliminate generic "one size fits all" review forms and processes.
    o   Create a performance improvement plan when someone needs to improve.

Now is the time to join the many organizations that are seeing the value of the most advanced performance appraisal and review software on the market. There is only one TIP to remove the stress from performance appraisals. With TIP the time needed to complete performance appraisals is reduced by up to 50%. There is no longer a need to put off performance appraisals until the last minute, because it only takes a few minutes to complete. With a few simply clicks of a mouse you are done with a review. This allows you to spend that quality time with the people and things that are really important and mean the most in life.

Watch the FREE guided demo to see just how much TIP can benefit your organization by visiting us online at www.tipsoftware.com or call us at 706-795-3557!

Notes